Praise for
The Fourth Fisherman

"Faith and hope unite the unlikely stories of Mexican fishermen lost at sea and an American television executive even more profoundly lost in his affluence. You'll be inspired by this passionate tale of intertwined lives, touched by the author's unvarnished honesty, and challenged to trust God in fresh ways. Here's an adventure story that may well launch you on your own new adventures with God."

—LEE STROBEL, *New York Times* best-selling author

"We love this message. Joe weaves together two stories with the same central theme, being lost and adrift, and tells how one thing—faith in God—provided each of the four fishermen the courage and comfort to face the next day and its uncertainties and ultimately led them safely to shore. These are the stories that we hold tight in our memories—when days seem so uncertain and doubts scream at us that we'll never find the shore."

—SHAUNTI and JEFF FELDHAHN, best-selling authors of
For Women Only and *For Men Only*

"This book is about the fishermen's agony and survival, or at least that's where Joe begins. But the real book, the inner story, shows readers how God took a once high-powered salesman who was obsessed with success and image and turned him into a new man: a dedicated husband and a serious, committed Christian."

—CECIL MURPHEY, *New York Times* best-selling coauthor of
90 Minutes in Heaven

"People of faith, myself included, often put limitations on it. But, as you'll read here, real freedom comes when we finally surrender to the mystery of God and what He is doing. Thank you, Joe, for being so honest and real. I loved it!"

—JEFF FOXWORTHY, stand-up comedian and television personality

"You won't be able to put this book down. It is more than the true story of three courageous fishermen and one brave author. Believe it or not, hidden within their inspiring stories is your story. It is the belief that life is bigger than we think. It is the hope of wanting our lives to have purpose. It's all there. If you're looking to find that hope, a common purpose, and a reason to still believe, you've come to the right place. But be warned. The journey begins when you board this boat."

—JEFF HENDERSON, North Point Ministries

"Joe is an ordinary guy who has been given an extraordinary story. He answered a call that few will ever get a chance to say yes to. I wish it could have been me."

—STEVE BARTKOWSKI, NFL legend, outdoorsman, and
    motivational speaker

THE
FOURTH
FISHERMAN

How Three Mexican Fishermen Who Came Back from the Dead
Changed My Life and Saved My Marriage

JOE
KISSACK

WATERBROOK
PRESS

THE FOURTH FISHERMAN
PUBLISHED BY WATERBROOK PRESS
12265 Oracle Boulevard, Suite 200
Colorado Springs, Colorado 80921

All Scripture quotations, unless otherwise indicated, are taken from the King James Version. Scripture quotations marked (MSG) are taken from The Message by Eugene H. Peterson. Copyright © 1993, 1994, 1995, 1996, 2000, 2001, 2002. Used by permission of NavPress Publishing Group. All rights reserved. Scripture quotations marked (NIV) are taken from the Holy Bible, New International Version®, NIV®. Copyright © 1973, 1978, 1984 by Biblica Inc.™ Used by permission of Zondervan. All rights reserved worldwide. www.zondervan.com.

Grateful acknowledgment is made to Ralf Hoppe of Der Spiegel for the information he provided regarding the fishermen and their story.

ISBN 978-0-307-95627-9
ISBN 978-0-307-95628-6 (electronic)

Cover design by Mark D. Ford

Published in the United States by WaterBrook Multnomah, an imprint of the Crown Publishing Group, a division of Random House Inc., New York.

WATERBROOK and its deer colophon are registered trademarks of Random House Inc.

Library of Congress Cataloging-in-Publication Data
Kissack, Joe.
    The fourth fisherman : how three Mexican fishermen who came back from the dead changed my life and saved my marriage / Joe Kissack. — 1st ed.
        p. cm.
    Includes bibliographical references (p.   ).
    ISBN 978-0-307-95627-9 — ISBN 978-0-307-95628-6 (electronic)
    1. Kissack, Joe. 2. Christian biography—United States. 3. Survival at sea—Pacific Ocean.
I. Title.
    BR1725.K498A3 2012
    277.3'083092—dc23
    [B]
                                    2011039575

Printed in the United States of America
2012—First Edition

10 9 8 7 6 5 4 3 2 1

SPECIAL SALES
Most WaterBrook Multnomah books are available at special quantity discounts when purchased in bulk by corporations, organizations, and special-interest groups. Custom imprinting or excerpting can also be done to fit special needs. For information, please e-mail SpecialMarkets@ WaterBrookMultnomah.com or call 1-800-603-7051.

To Carmen

She endures

Contents

1. RED CARPET

I f something dark was looming, I wasn't aware of it. Not yet. Not now. I stood on the red carpet at the Emmy Awards, wearing obscenely expensive sunglasses. It was September of 1997, and my employment contract with Columbia TriStar Television was about to expire. I'd been invited to fly out to L.A. for some important meetings that would determine the next move in my soaring career. A seat at the Emmys was an extra perk, a glamour ticket in Hollywood.

I certainly looked the part: a thousand-dollar tuxedo, cuff links from Neiman Marcus, a Rolex Oyster Day-Date, Ferragamo shoes, and, of course, those sunglasses—three hundred bucks' worth of eye candy.

I had "arrived" according to Hollywood's standards, often calculated by one's ability to spend outrageous amounts of money on items of little substance. Even knowing that, I was a repeat offender. And I loved every glistening gold dollar of this good life. After all, I'd earned it. In my tenth year with a major television studio that had promoted me five times, I'd climbed all the way to executive vice president, pulling down a big salary with incredible bonuses. My job allowed for marvelous vacations, dining in the best restaurants, and shopping at the coolest boutiques. I always traveled first class (concierge level, of course), and I received a car allowance that paid for my BMW 540i and later my Porsche 911 Carrera Cabriolet. I owned a six-thousand-square-foot house, complete with a home theater and sound system that would straighten the hair on your legs. And, oh yes, I rode a Harley-Davidson—just because I could.

If I saw something I liked, I bought it. If something could make me look better, I got it. If a hotel wasn't up to my standards, I found a better one. It was all about having the best. Not bad for a small-town kid from a blue-collar family in Illinois whose daughters make fun of him for having worn the same plaid shirt in his first- and second-grade class photos! Standing on the red carpet was an exclamation-point celebration of a once-lost kid who now looked so sharp.

Of course, there was something else. My life was furiously driven by something deep beneath the surface. Something I didn't know that I didn't know.

Trying to survive in the television industry is like being on the TV show *Survivor.* You're on a team, but the truth is, it's every man for himself. With an average of four shows to pitch each year, I was giving more than a thousand presentations annually. It wasn't brainiac stuff, but it was incredibly nerve-racking. I had to be "on" all the time; tens of millions of dollars were riding on it. Sure, some days it was glamorous, but the second I closed a deal, I would start stressing about the next one. I felt only as good as the last big thing I landed. This despite some of my successes—*Married...with Children; Mad About You; Walker, Texas Ranger; Ricki Lake.* Of course, there was also that big one—*Seinfeld.*

My job was to license the rights of television programs to broadcast stations across the country, otherwise known as syndication. Whoever figured out that television audiences would watch the same program a second, third, or even seventeenth time was a genius. Syndication is highly profitable—and cutthroat. With only so many clients in each city and twenty other shows competing for the same limited time slots, it's impossible to sell your show in every market. The expectation, however, is that you will. Every major studio had more than a dozen of us hired guns. We traveled to all 211 TV markets, four days a week, fifty weeks a year, from New York City all the way to Glendive, Montana, and every trip was destined, on some level, to fail.

But—and this is a big *but*—the money was fabulous. And most of us hired guns lived beyond our means, believing that as long as the money was coming in, the physical and emotional toll was worth it. Believe me, it is very difficult to walk away.

Much as I reveled in my red-carpet moment, I knew it was just another part of the dance. The invitation—the whole weekend for that matter—was one more perk the studio had pushed in front of me, knowing I wouldn't, or couldn't, refuse their pot of gold at the end of the rainbow. It was all calculated. They had me right where they wanted me. I was a guy once obsessed with a worn-out plaid shirt, who hailed from a town whose chief industries were canning peas and spinning yarn, and now I was raking in lots of dough (and needing it to keep up my lifestyle), rubbing elbows with American entertainment royalty, and looking like a million bucks.

One of the keys to successful red-carpet walking is to do it slowly, especially the final twenty yards before you get inside. The proper walk is important, because you're supposed to project an aura of appreciation tinged with indifference, but never gratitude and certainly not awe. As an old coach once told me, "Joe, if you're lucky enough to wind up in the end zone, act like you've been there before." I played the part pretty well. I had rehearsed for this moment endlessly. I knew how to cruise through a five-star hotel lobby and into a waiting limousine with just enough mystery that I looked like I could be somebody famous.

Illusion is important in Hollywood. It's carefully crafted on-screen; it's carefully cultivated offscreen. I'd gotten the hang of it.

There on the red carpet, my lovely wife, Carmen, stood by my side, just as she had during my entire climb up the professional ladder. She was a rock and looked like a rock star. Among many things, she was an incredible mother and kept the family running like a finely tuned machine. "Very special," her dad once told me, as tears welled up in his eyes. "That Carmen... she is a special one."

Even though Carmen's presence helped me project my grand illusion before the eyes of others, she was skeptical of the life I'd pursued. She had seen the wear and tear resulting from the demands of the job and tried to suggest that I needed more balance in my life. Carmen feared that I was being ground down to nothing and didn't understand why I kept renewing my contract. She would encourage me with her cheerleader smile, attempting to give me confidence. "Joe, you're a talented guy. You can do other things..." But I was like a suicide bomber who didn't have the wires connected quite right, and I was determined about my mission. Even if it killed me.

I suppose I knew that I was pushing too hard. Earlier that week I had met with the head of television for the studio, and he asked me the classic interview question: "Where do you see yourself five, ten, or fifteen years from now?" I told him bluntly I wanted his job someday. It was positively ludicrous to think I could handle this guy's responsibilities. He was ridiculously smart and operated as if ice water ran through his veins. It sounded good when I said it, though, and it was probably what he wanted to hear. Again, illusion.

I knew I was driven. But I had to be. The industry was intense: the farther you advanced up the ladder, the fewer the jobs—very few lateral moves. It was all about the next job, and there were only about six jobs at my level in the entire studio system. There was no workplace Zen back then. It was all tension, all the time. If you weren't stressed and strung out, you would be replaced. Some guys could handle it—thousands of canned speeches, smiles, fake laughter, and contracts. I felt I could too. I was holding it all together. Besides, everything I held dear was riding on my ability to continue to climb, to succeed: my house, my car, my family's future, my reputation. My sunglasses. The moment I stepped off that tightrope, it would all be gone, handed to the next guy in line. Every day on the job at the studio was, to my mind, another day I might be found out.

Some years before, to deal with the stress, I had tried seeing a shrink. There I'd learned a few things about myself, primarily that I had equated my success and lifestyle with my value as a husband, father, and head of household. I suppose I was looking for validation, approval, something to fill me up.

At one point the psychiatrist looked into my eyes and said, "Tell me about your father." No one had ever gone there before, and I didn't know what to say. So I never went back. I didn't want, nor could I even begin, to have a conversation about my father. Not with anyone.

Really, it wasn't such a big deal, or so I thought. Everyone was chasing something they wanted, the good life they desired, the status that would garner respect. I was no different. What if there were stresses? I just needed to manage them better.

And I felt I had. Look where I was! The sun was shining. Carmen was by my side. I was at the Emmys in Hollywood, about to re-up with my studio. I had made a name for myself.

We turned and began our slow, convincing stroll into the Pasadena Civic Auditorium for the commencement of the ceremonies. Yet, walking through all that dazzle and glitter, I could not see on the horizon the storm that was about to engulf my life. Through my sunglasses, the world looked sunny and rosy. But behind those lenses, my eyes betrayed lines of anxiety, worry, and stress.

We are so blind to our own stuff, blind to the storm bearing down on us. In fact, I was already adrift. I just didn't know it.

2. THE FISHERMEN

Shortly before sunrise on October 28, 2005, five fishermen prepared to launch a twenty-seven-foot fiberglass boat along the shore of San Blas, a small sea town on the western coast of Mexico. This boat, resembling an oversized skiff, was called a *panga*.

The marina cove was filled with hundreds of these little boats, tied to tree limbs that had been pushed into the ocean floor as makeshift dock cleats. There were no real docks, just one insignificant boat after another attached by any means possible to tree limbs jutting out of the water. The shoreline consisted of three-foot-high grass littered with rusted-out containers, oil barrels, chairs, doors, and other trash. Farther down the shoreline, dozens of sunken boats, lame and listing, lay dead as if they had done their service in war and washed up onshore after a great battle.

The captain of the panga, Juan David Lorenzo, had assembled his crew just the day before. Consequently, most of these men didn't know each other, and they remained quiet and kept to themselves as they stocked the boat with what they would need for the trip. Lorenzo, known to the men as "Señor

Juan," was not a professional fisherman but owned a boat, an engine, and a fishing net, all of which made him captain.

With luck, they would fish the boat full in three days. Just to be safe, they packed enough sandwiches, canned tuna, and bottled water to last four days, along with some blankets and extra clothes. A day's worth of fishing might yield each man two hundred pesos, about twenty dollars. Three days would give each man enough to live meagerly for about a week.

A husky man in his forties, Señor Juan was adept at repairing computers and installing networks. He had held such a job in Mazatlán, but his real passion always led him to the water, down to San Blas. More than anything he was an adventurer. The ocean fascinated him. Fishing was fun, but just a pastime; he simply loved being on the water in his boat.

Fishing was for Señor Juan a hobby, but for Salvador Ordoñez it was his life. Ordoñez had been a fisherman for nearly thirty years, having learned to fish on the east coast of Mexico in the Gulf. He had started fishing for sharks in his teens and ended up in San Blas fifteen years ago.

Señor Juan knew he needed a crew who not only had fishing expertise but who also were as tough as nails in order to handle the hard work that fishing in this part of the world requires. To him, being tough was important on the water and also in life. Macho was what he wanted himself to be; it was also what he looked for in others. On the ocean they would not use fishing rods but rather a net that took much strength to toss out and especially to pull in. Three or four days on the ocean under the sun took its physical toll. You had to be tough, Señor Juan knew, and Salvador Ordoñez was certainly that.

Two other crew members, Lucio and Jesús, brought to the crew their own scrappy machismo and fishing experience.

Lucio Rendon was the tallest of the five and looked like a Mayan warrior. He'd grown up the hard way. He had lived in a small dirt-floor hut with his grandmother, whom he called Panchita, since he was ten years old. Lucio had quit school at thirteen and learned from his uncle Remigio how to fish.

Fishing became his life. Lucio typically walked or hitched rides to the nearest fishing village, Boca del Asadero, and would be gone for days or weeks at a time, looking to pick up jobs as a day laborer on the water.

Lucio often had a soft and sad look about him, even when he was smiling, as though he had just gotten some disappointing news. It was perhaps the effect of a hard life and its resulting weariness even though he was still a young man.

Like Lucio, Jesús Vidana moved from town to town in search of work on small fishing boats. He lived eight hours north of San Blas in a one-room shack that he built out of sticks and scraps of lumber. The shack had no electricity or running water, and the interior walls were covered with cardboard for insulation. Jesús was married and lived with his pregnant wife, Jocelyn, and their son, Juan, almost three. On extremely hot nights, Jesús cooled off his family with an electric fan that he ran off a hundred-foot extension cord stretching to his nearest neighbor's house.

Jesús was always full of energy, "passion" as he would call it, which kept him constantly smiling and laughing and brought a smile to the people who knew him well. But his passion would sometimes turn in another direction and puff him up like a Texas horned frog, warning an approaching predator to think twice about messing with him. Yet, unlike the lizard, Jesús wouldn't spit blood from his eyes. He was more bark than bite.

Señor Juan looked around anxiously in the predawn. Wanting them to get away before it was light, he urged the men to hurry. He was often headstrong, sometimes baring a temper, and he would make a crew perform quickly. Anyone who saw the hundreds of fishing boats in the cove would soon know, as he did, that fishing on the Pacific in pangas was a common way of life. Like everyone around him, he had done this many times. Yet he didn't take anything for granted. While routine, it was still dangerous work, and he needed the right crew members, ones he could count on to handle what was always a hard job.

Señor Juan had handpicked the fifth man, whom he had known previously. His name was Farsero. To Señor Juan, Farsero was a dependable crew member. To the others, he was a mystery. They didn't know much about him, and he never volunteered anything about himself. When someone would ask about his life, he would say, "You don't need to know." Señor Juan had introduced him to the other men as *El Farsero,* which means "the Joker." Thing was, he rarely smiled.

But then, each of the men had something, something unique, even mysterious. An untold story, a passion, a special ability. Lucio had actually known Salvador from a previous fishing job. Lucio didn't talk about it, but a year earlier the engine on their boat had failed, and they'd been stranded on an island for a period of time. Jesús had an incredible singing voice that could gloriously fill the air out of nowhere. And Salvador, tough and rugged, had a deep faith in God. One of the last things he carried into the panga was his prized possession. His Bible.

The panga had a V-shaped hull that was nine feet wide and five feet deep, with four three-foot-tall dividers that split the interior into five sections. There was a partially covered area in the bow for storage. In addition to a few tools, food, blankets, and extra clothes, they had on board an ice-filled cooler, shark knives, a whetstone, some rope, and an anchor. This particular panga had an added feature: a welded flotation chamber that provided extra buoyancy so the craft could carry a larger load of fish.

As day broke behind them, the five fishermen headed past the harbor master's shack and out of the channel. Señor Juan turned the panga west toward the Islas Marías, which lay sixty miles ahead. He gunned the engine, and the front end of the boat rose out of the calm Pacific waters. Being at the helm, in control, gave him a rush.

The other four men nestled against the inner walls of the boat, preparing for a long ride, not expecting what the day would actually bring.

3. THE PADDLE

Go get me the paddle," my dad would say.

Only we weren't going canoeing. I never expected to hear that sentence. I don't know why, because after a while I should have been able to figure out when it was coming. But somehow it always surprised me.

I was about nine years old when the paddlings started, usually over some innocuous incident typical of a kid my age, like telling a fib, throwing a tantrum, or spelling my name on the driveway with butane and setting it on fire. And, okay, there was that time when I was five that I stabbed my brother in the leg with a pair of scissors. (I had no idea that leg skin was so soft.)

In our house, discipline was doled out with my dad's fraternity paddle, which lived on top of the refrigerator next to the dust bunnies and cigarettes and vodka until summoned into action, usually about ten or twelve times a year. When he said those five words, it was as though he were asking someone to pass the salt. The request didn't seem to carry any anger. It scared the daylights out of me, but I don't think it affected him at all. His face was expressionless, and he didn't look at me when he said it.

I think I started to learn how to mask the pain after I got the paddle from the fridge for the very first time. I sent myself off in my own little world, adrift in the shame of his words and confused by it all.

Struggling to numb myself, I tried everything—rerunning episodes of *Hogan's Heroes* or *The Munsters* in my head and playing imaginary games of basketball where every shot went in—to convince myself that the pain was only temporary. Whatever it took, I did it.

"Assume the position," he would command. He was like an executioner who had no connection to his victims and was purposely and permanently detached from his actions.

I would start to reach my hands down toward my feet.

"Bend over and grab your ankles." Sadly, I learned what an ankle was by experiencing this humiliating routine countless times. By the time I was grabbing them, I couldn't feel a thing.

Neither of us spoke during these sessions. The only sound was my dad paddling me. His goal was to impress upon me not only certain letters of the Greek alphabet that the fraternity paddle bore but also our family's cardinal rule: *never mess up.*

Photos of my father when he was a kid show a serious little boy dressed in overalls. Even today, seeing these images of him with his mother and father, with stern looks on their faces, sends me guessing at the puzzle of his life. Perhaps it was a belt or a switch lashing his behind at the hands of a giant, angry father. Maybe that's where the silence came from. Addiction. Anger. Bitterness. No one seems to know the details, but something must have caused the man great pain. It has manifested itself in so many ways.

I think I had it easier than my older brothers and my sister. They endured a less-mellow version of my father and grew great, ugly tumors of loathing for a man who even now remains mostly oblivious to the pain and damage he caused. I was the baby: strong, agreeable, and apparently full of promise to a dad hellbent on raising a quarterback. I was competitive too, adding my name to the roster of every sports league my little town had to offer, partly to please my father but mostly for the opportunity to hit back, to rage and rush and pound in ways legitimized by a referee and uniforms. Football was ideal for this. I wanted to be a linebacker like Dick Butkus.

Unfortunately, I was told I had to be a quarterback. *Quarterback? No, please not quarterback. They don't get to hit people.* Fran Tarkenton was a quarterback. And what's more, he was a *scrambling* quarterback; he actually ran *away* from people. I didn't want to be Fran Tarkenton. I wanted to be Dick Butkus. I wanted to pile into someone and drive him into the ground. It was my chance to prove my manhood, to be macho, to take my anger at my dad out on others.

Well, I was a lousy quarterback. Everyone knew it, especially my dad, who rarely missed a chance to remind me. But I was good at making people laugh, which was a great way to hide the mess inside. So I mostly hung out with people who got my jokes or didn't mind being the butt of them. When I was with them, I could feel good enough, even if it was only for a few minutes at the lunch table.

In that tiny town, you didn't hate your father. Or if you did, you never said so. You went out for football, kept your nose to the grindstone, and, if you were lucky, got a good job at the yarn factory. I continued to defend him to the rest of my family and the town at large for the longest time, as sons who long for their fathers' approval tend to do.

In some ways he was like many other dads. He was a small-town baseball, football, and basketball coach who wanted his kids to be winners. He worked hard; he was a carpenter in the summers. But I guess everything looked like a nail to him, and he was the hammer. I just never knew which side of him was going to show up on any given day.

He tried to connect with me through golf. One time in high school, I was winning a match in the club championship. I was up by three holes with four left to play when he came out on the course and started to tell me I wasn't doing something right. I asked him to leave, and he got angry and stormed off. I lost the match on the final hole. That night after a few too many, he stormed into the family room, swinging. I put my arms around my head, like a boxer who is just trying to survive the round. My mom had been cutting his hair and was right on his tail, holding a pair of scissors like a switchblade, trying to protect me. He popped me a few times, and my mom started yelling that she was calling the police. All I remember is that he stopped.

I know I'm not the only kid who was beaten by his father. And, like others who've experienced the same thing, the ultimate escape was, well, escape. Perhaps you know this all too well. Perhaps you left. You left home and went elsewhere—to college, on a trip, to a job across country. Distance faded the feelings, the memories. And eventually you built a new life in which you did something else, something you were successful at.

Even so, those experiences are still inside you. And what you do each week, each day, is somehow touched by them. Only you don't know it. You don't know why you do what you do.

I remember when I was seventeen, just before I left home for good, my dad started taking me with him on his motorcycle trips—an attempt, I suppose, at father-son bonding. We would ride out on the new blacktop, stop at every white-trash bar along the way, and sit together in silence while I perfected a new way to cover up my pain: popping top after top of Old Milwaukee until I was numb. Then we would ride home. Ironically, he had shattered his paddle on my callused behind a year earlier, beating me for the very thing he was now encouraging. All of a sudden I was his drinking buddy.

During the beatings I had done my best to escape the pain by drifting into an imaginary world in my mind. Later, after I had experienced the effect of alcohol hitting my stomach, my escape route was a great deal faster, was much more effective, and took considerably less effort. Oh, the things we don't know about the things we don't know.

I was very unclear about who I was supposed to be, where I was supposed to be headed. But I left, nonetheless, setting out on some ocean of life, chasing after something I was supposed to achieve.

4. THE PACIFIC

When the panga neared the Islas Marías, Señor Juan cut the engine. The men immediately began to unfurl the fishing net, the *cimbra,* as they had done hundreds of times.

A cimbra is made by hand from fine but strong nylon fibers. It is strung between two poles, and the younger boys in the fishing villages walk back and forth, weaving it together like a giant, milelong tennis net. It floats horizontally about twenty feet below the surface of the water, suspended by beat-up buoys that have flagsticks attached to them to signal other boats to steer clear. Once the net is in place, the boat slowly zigzags across the water, snagging any sea life that happens to be in the wrong place at the wrong time.

This particular cimbra extended for nearly two miles.

Señor Juan valued his cimbra as much as his boat. The huge net was worth three thousand dollars, more than a year's wages for a fisherman. It was so prized that one would risk his life to save it. Occasionally something will get caught in a cimbra that could damage it. A stingray, for example, can shred a cimbra in a short time. In such a case, a fisherman will take off all his clothes, grab a shark knife, dive into the water, and slice off the "wings" of the animal with surgical precision even as the stingray is trying to kill him—all to prevent damage to the net.

Attached to the bottom edge of the cimbra and spaced about every thirty feet, ten-foot-long wires carry three-inch shark hooks sometimes baited with fish. On the surface above each shark line, a float—usually a plastic soft-drink bottle—serves as a marker. When a fisherman sees any sort of commotion in the net, he pulls the net toward the boat. If there is something of value, say a shark or a tuna, he'll yank it out of the net, throw it in the belly of the boat, and hit it on the head with a club.

This is backbreaking work.

The first day out, the unsuspecting five fishermen caught nothing of consequence. After the cimbra was in place, they sat on the boat, waiting for action in the net, dozing off occasionally when there was none.

Most fishermen in this part of the world have been doing this since second grade. Their fathers do this. Their brothers do this. Their sisters are married to men who do this. Uncles, grandfathers, great-grandfathers—all the men as far back as they can remember—have done this. Mostly, they sit and wait and watch the markers for any movement. Sometimes they make small talk; sometimes they doze off. When nature calls, they relieve themselves by hanging off the back of the boat and dragging their butts in the water. No paper required.

Just past midnight a shift in the wind woke Salvador, also known by the familiar name "Chava." Moving rapidly toward them was a wall of black clouds five miles high. Salvador woke the other men, but Señor Juan and Farsero were unconcerned about the approaching storm. It was as if the two of them had never been in this kind of situation before and couldn't fathom its seriousness.

Jesús and Lucio were alert and standing by, like policemen backing up a fellow officer in trouble. They were ready to burst into action when called upon. They knew the seriousness of the situation. Even though they were only in their midtwenties and might seem like a couple of wandering day laborers, each had been doing this kind of work for nearly twenty years. They were experienced and as tough as they come, and they knew the situation could get bad really quickly.

Within a few minutes the wind was howling and quickly escalated to forty miles per hour, producing fifteen-foot swells that tossed the boat and its contents around like Ping-Pong balls in a lottery drawing. Flashes of lightning lit up the night sea.

They squatted down low against the side of the boat to secure themselves. Cold seawater came blasting across the boat and rushed at them with crushing blows, stabbing their eyes like needles.

Salvador knew that each monstrous wave carried the threat of death. If the panga were to capsize or if the men were swept overboard, there was little chance they would survive. One swell lifted the boat thirty feet high and brought it down with a thunderous crash, stretching the cimbra beyond its breaking point and snapping the line like a ripe string bean.

"Why didn't you tie the line right?" Señor Juan screamed at Salvador.

"You're the captain!" he responded angrily. "You should have checked it yourself." Salvador stood in the center of the boat, up to his chest in icy seawater, his eyes burning.

Salvador always gave respect to those in authority…if they earned it. On the sea, anyone can be called "captain." Owning a boat might get you *called* a captain, but it doesn't *make* you one. Blaming or shaming the crew wasn't going to make Señor Juan captain.

The ugly black waves kept pushing them twenty and thirty feet into the air and into icy foam at the top. Then, like a roller coaster getting reacquainted with gravity, the boat would drop straight down into the darkness. There was nothing for them to do but hold on to the top edge of the side of the panga and hope she stayed upright.

They gathered as much strength as possible and jockeyed through the anger of the sea, watching most of their supplies fly out into the blackness. It was like going twelve rounds with Mike Tyson. An angry Mike Tyson.

The storm finally subsided.

And the fishermen took stock of what had happened. The cimbra was nowhere in sight. A tattered rope was all that remained.

"We will find the net," growled Señor Juan.

Salvador tried to reason with him, suggesting they try to reach land and come back later to look for the net, but Señor Juan refused.

Salvador was an experienced fisherman—nearly thirty years' worth—and he had seen this happen before. Equipment often gets lost, and sometimes the best thing to do is to go to shore, get some rest, and come back later with a fresh set of eyes and more cans of gasoline. He wasn't telling Señor Juan to go to shore for his own selfish reasons. He sincerely wanted to help Señor Juan find his net, and Salvador knew that taking a break was an intelligent solution.

But Señor Juan insisted on continuing the search. Salvador deferred to the authority of Señor Juan as the owner of the boat, and he stayed alert, diligently looking for the lost cimbra. They remained on the water for two more days as Señor Juan frantically circled and crisscrossed the area, nearly exhausting their fuel supply.

Salvador knew that getting back to land was now going to be impossible. They didn't have enough fuel. He knew the only thing they could do was look for another boat. They eventually spotted a vessel in the distance and headed for it.

All the men felt relieved. Even though they hadn't found the net, at least they had found someone who could help them get to land so they could refuel and come back the next day to continue the search.

But before they got halfway there, the engine sputtered and died. They had drained the gas cans. The men shouted and waved at the other boat, still a half mile away. But perhaps not wanting to get their fishing lines tangled, the men in the other boat started their engine and pulled away. No other boats were in sight. Most had returned to port ahead of the storm. The panga was drifting now, caught in the westward-moving Pacific current. Tempers began to flare.

Salvador could still see one of the Marías Islands, but the strong current was pushing their small fishing boat out to sea.

The fishermen soon realized that the missing cimbra was the least of their problems. The storm had washed away some of the tools and all the canned food. A few bottles of water and a couple of sandwiches remained, along with their shark knives, some extra clothes, a few blankets, and Salvador's Bible.

After the two days of searching for the cimbra, the men were exhausted and finally couldn't help but fall asleep.

When Salvador opened his eyes the next morning, he stood up and looked around. He saw nothing but water in every direction.

5. THE CAMPUS

The first time I saw Carmen, she was wearing blood-red penny loafers, a yellow button-down shirt, and khakis. She was stunning. Her brown, sun-bleached hair was cut very short, and her features were sharp and strong.

I didn't hear or see anything else.

I watched her glide across the room and, to my dismay, sit next to my six-foot-four, 280-pound roommate, Pee-Wee. He and I were going into our senior year and were part of a group of University of Iowa students who had volunteered to help returning alumni have a good time at their class reunion. I figured it would be a good addition to my résumé, and I could use the free yellow shirt they gave us.

I was just about to jump across the table and force myself between this ravishing mystery girl and Pee-Wee when he mumbled something to her that made her laugh. *Oh no.* He said something else to her. She laughed again. I was ready to hit the panic button. One more joke from him and I would be toast. It didn't help that he was rather good-looking. I sat there plotting my strategy. *How am I going to wedge myself between them?* When the meeting was over, Pee-Wee hustled out the door with her in a flash. By the time I got to the hallway, they were nowhere to be found.

"Another One Bites the Dust" played in my head until I got home that night. I was consoling myself with my daily Little Debbie bar when Pee-Wee walked into our apartment.

"You know that girl I left the meeting with?" he said casually. "She wanted to know if I knew the guy with 'the dreamy brown eyes.'"

What? Can it be? Yes! She was talking about me!

I sat him down and interrogated him. "Where is she from?" "How old is she?" "What's she like?" "C'mon, man! I need this information!" A few days later I spotted the short-haired beauty I thought I had lost to the big fella. She was with her roommate, Leigh Ann, but all I could see was Carmen. I walked over and stood in their path.

"I'm going to marry you," I blurted out, surprising even myself.

"I don't even know you," Carmen said.

"Well, why don't you go out with me and get to know me?" I asked.

"I have a boyfriend," she said, which momentarily threw me off stride.

"Oh," I said, trying to disguise the angst I was feeling. I vaguely remember saying something along the lines of "I guess I'll see you around, then" and walked off.

But having been so close to her, I knew that somehow, boyfriend or not, I had to find a way to make her mine. I asked my friend Kevin, a budding investigative journalist, to track down Carmen's phone number. He came back with Leigh Ann's number instead, so I called her, gave her my number, and asked her to put in a good word about me to Carmen.

In spite of my attempted preempt—"I'm going to marry you"—Carmen called me back and agreed to have drinks with me. (For the record, I had never used that line on any other girl.)

The day after our first date, she told me she liked my sense of humor, and later she told me she was disappointed that I hadn't kissed her good night. The truth is, I didn't want to scare her off, so I went the other direction entirely: completely hands (and lips) off. I was out of my mind in love.

I waited two excruciating days and called to see if we could get together again. This time we kissed. It was skyrockets in flight.

But there was one problem: her boyfriend. She really did have one. He was handsome and ripped. I weighed 147 pounds dripping wet. During the weeks after I first met Carmen, we saw each other sporadically. One night while on a walk, we stopped by a park and strolled over to the swings. While we were swinging, I decided to deliver an ultimatum.

"I don't want you to date anyone else," I said firmly. I actually was expecting to hear the worst: "You seem like a really nice guy, but…" or "I think we should just be friends" or, worst of all, "I'm sorry. I was about to tell you that I just got engaged."

I waited for her response.

"I broke up with him today," she said with little fanfare. My ears must have been on a tape delay, because I barged right ahead. "There is just no way I can continue to see you if you won't see me exclusively—"

Wait. Did she just say that she broke up with him today? For me? Before I even asked her to?

Yes, indeed.

After that, we went everywhere and did everything together. I suppose we were destined to be married. All I thought about was how much I wanted to be with Carmen. She was warm, muffiny goodness, and I felt loved, maybe for the first time in my life. And besides, she laughed at my shtick. Having a beautiful girl love you and laugh at your jokes is about all a guy really needs.

It certainly soothed a host of personal wounds. The humiliation of the beatings, the piercing of the shame, and the confusion about where I was going and who I was supposed to be—all faded. Her presence in my life gave me a sense of equilibrium I'd never had before.

Fall semester had started, and it seemed to us that it was time for me to meet her parents. Well, really it was Carmen's idea; I'm pretty sure I was more than willing to put that off. But we drove from Iowa City to her hometown of Newton on a Friday to see her brother play in a high-school football game. And I met her mom and dad, which went just fine. (At least they didn't act bothered by my being there.)

Carmen and I went to the country club where she had been a lifeguard. We visited her high school and later saw some of her old friends. We drove by the Maytag washer-and-dryer factory, then went to the Maid-Rite, where we ate loose-meat sandwiches, and finally ended up at the appliance store her mom and dad owned. It was like that John Cougar Mellencamp song: "Ain't that America for you and me... Little pink houses..."

I had two job offers out of college: Maytag and the Carnation Milk Company. Maytag was based in Carmen's hometown, so we quickly crossed that one off the list, because we knew we would wind up together, and she didn't want to live so close to her parents' home. Carnation offered me a job in Charlotte, and I said yes.

Man, I had hit it big. More than $19,500 a year and a company car (a two-year-old Chevy Citation). Three brand-new suits from Ewers Men's Store (I had worked there while I was in college), two pairs of wingtips (one black, one brown), and a Sears credit card. I thought I was rich, hauling in that $19,500. It seemed enough to buy anything and everything I could ever want. (It took me a few years to pay off the Sears card. That vacuum cleaner wound up costing me about 700 bucks.)

Carmen and I had a great summer together. But summer ended, and she had to go back to school for her senior year. And when she left, I was a mess.

I was terrible at my job, and I wasn't too fond of my boss, who thought he was General Patton. And I was very lonely.

I had only two friends, Pat and Greg. They were fun guys who worked in the television business, and they invited me to do stuff with them, mostly stuff that involved drinking beer.

I'd call Carmen every few days in tears and beg her to visit me. She would come for the weekend, and when she went home, I would cling to Pat and Greg. One Saturday afternoon we carried Pat's TV down to the pool and watched football all day. While drinking and watching TV, I had to study my product line because General Patton would be quizzing me on Monday about the price of a six-ounce can versus a ten-ounce can of Mighty Dog.

"Hey, you might be good at what Greg and I do," Pat said out of the blue. "We sell TV time."

"TV time?" I loved TV. TV sets. TV commercials. TV dinners. *I can do anything that has anything to do with TV,* I thought.

He set up an interview for me, and I put on my best suit and the black wingtips. They had really cool offices near the mall, and his company car was a Cutlass Ciera. Man, what I wouldn't do to have a Ciera!

His boss said they might have an opening in Atlanta. One day the next week I drove there to meet the manager, who said I seemed like the "right cut of cloth." He must have liked my blue suit and my wingtips. Two weeks later I moved to Atlanta.

I was finally on my way.

6. Blood Brothers

The fishermen had been drifting for about four days.

All the food and water was gone. Jesús's last supper was whatever he could squeeze from his tube of toothpaste the night before.

"We have God above us, watching over us," Salvador told the others, trying to reassure them. He was confident they would survive. "He is always with us. We have a Bible. We have to pray."

Salvador's Bible was special to him. When he was a young man, he had often gotten into trouble. During one of those escapades, a friend of his was badly injured. The doctor said he would never walk again. Every day while he was in the hospital, Salvador's friend read the Bible his parents had given him. He told Salvador he had confessed his wrongdoing to God, had promised to do his best in the future, and trusted that God was going to perform a miracle. He believed he would walk out of the hospital on his own two legs. Salvador agreed that this would be a great blessing, but he watched his friend endure weeks of physical therapy without any progress.

When the day came to leave the hospital, Salvador's friend rolled himself toward the exit in a rickety old wheelchair. Suddenly one of the wheels came off, stopping the chair dead in its tracks. Salvador watched in amazement as his friend lifted himself out of the chair, took a step toward the door, and walked out of the hospital just as he had said he would. The friend told Salvador that if he would believe in the power of God, miracles were available for him. He handed his Bible to Salvador as a gift.

The other men did not know the story of Salvador's Bible, and Señor Juan did not appear to share Salvador's faith. He sat against the edge of the boat for hours on end, doing very little. Farsero often mimicked Señor Juan's pouting.

Salvador was slowly becoming the captain by default, Jesús his second in command, and Lucio a sometime helper and official timekeeper because he had a twenty-dollar Casio watch with a day-date calendar. On the first night after they realized they were lost, Lucio looked at the watch. It was ten minutes to seven. After what felt like two hours had passed, he looked at it again. It was five minutes to seven.

Salvador assigned the men jobs that could help them pass the time and give them a sense of purpose. Jesús and Lucio were to watch for passing boats. Two days later they spotted two enormous oil tankers on the horizon and started yelling and waving their arms. All the men took off their shirts and waved them furiously, screaming at the top of their lungs. They had no doubt that someone on one of the tankers would see them. But even if someone had been looking for a small boat, it would have been impossible to see it from that distance.

Going for days without water was making it difficult for the men to swallow. It felt as if they were ingesting tiny shards of glass. Several of the men considered seawater as their only option, but Salvador, who had taken a survival course a year earlier in San Blas, knew better. He told them it would be a mistake. Still, the others decided to take their chances. They dipped their shirts into the water, lifted them over their open mouths, and wrung out some of the seawater onto their tongues.

Meanwhile, Salvador cut off a chunk of a plastic container with a shark knife to make a cup. Then he lowered his pants.

"What are you doing?" asked Jesús in disbelief.

"I want to live," responded Salvador. "I am going to drink this—to survive." Salvador relieved himself into the cup, raised it to his lips, and drank.

"I'm not drinking mine!" said Lucio, laughing.

It wasn't long before Lucio and Jesús suffered the effects of drinking the seawater. Lucio described the pain as being stuck in the back and head with thousands of needles. His stomach ached so badly at times that he cried.

Realizing they could not drink any more seawater and that Salvador was right, Lucio and Jesús followed suit and began to drink their own urine.

Fortunately, the fishermen soon found themselves covered by a misty drizzle, and they created a makeshift gutter system off the bow enclosure, washing out empty gasoline containers to collect as much rainwater as they could.

They took turns sleeping during the day under the protection of the bow enclosure or under blankets. At night they could see the lights of ships miles in the distance, but it was useless to try to signal them. They occasionally would hear an aircraft overhead, but there was no chance that anyone gazing out a window from thirty thousand feet, even on a clear day, would see them.

The men often wondered if anyone back home had noticed they were missing. It wasn't unusual for them to be out of touch with their families for extended periods. Lucio's uncle Remigio, however, did go to San Blas and asked if anyone had seen his nephew lately. He also checked with San Blas harbor officials, who said they had no record of a boat leaving with Lucio on board. "Of course there isn't a record," Remigio told them. "They would have snuck out in the dark, because they were too poor to buy a fishing permit." The authorities said they would do what they could, but they weren't going to waste fuel looking for him on the water when it was just as likely that Lucio was spending a few days partying with friends, which he would do on occasion.

Señor Juan was still technically in charge, but Salvador was the one leading the effort to stay alive. Without food or regular water, the only constant source of nourishment on the boat was the Bible. Salvador read it regularly and offered it to the other men. It took a few attempts, but eventually the others found it could sustain them as well.

Jesús had hope. He repeated over and over that they would soon be rescued. But Lucio was becoming angry at everything, especially the boats that didn't see them. It had only been a couple of weeks, but he was starting to come unhinged. Thirteen days with no food and very little water was wearing on all the men, but when the temperature cooled down in the evenings, they would wake up and make small talk. Even though Señor Juan had tried to deflect blame for the loss of the cimbra, the other men forgave him for using up all the fuel searching for it. They understood that the net was very valuable and that, as captain and owner of the boat, he had the right to give the orders. Besides, it wasn't going to do anybody any good to harbor ill feelings. Salvador could see that Señor Juan was suffering more than the rest, so he made a special effort to comfort him.

One evening Salvador moved to the back of the boat where Señor Juan was leaning against the side, staring into the water.

"Chava, look," Señor Juan whispered, pointing to a spot in the sea twenty feet away. "*A caguama.*" In a flash Salvador was out of the boat and in the water. Startled by the splash, Lucio and Jesús rushed to the back of the boat to see what was happening. Farsero didn't move. Salvador grabbed hold of the shell of a forty-pound sea turtle. He had done this sort of thing before but never in a weakened state from two weeks without food and never in a current that was moving faster than he could swim. He knew that if he got too far from the boat, he wouldn't be able to make it back. Salvador also knew that the turtle was about to dive hard.

He tried to flip the turtle over, but before he could, the turtle took him for a ride eight feet below the water. When he and the turtle resurfaced, Salvador kicked his legs frantically, trying to get back to the boat, still clutching the shell. Jesús and Lucio cheered him on, waiting with shark knives and what was left of the tattered rope that had held the cimbra.

Finally, Salvador pushed the turtle to the edge of the boat, and Lucio looped the rope around one of its front flippers. Jesús grabbed the other flipper, and they lifted their next meal into the boat. Then they reached down and pulled in Salvador.

Jesús sliced off a flipper and gave it to Salvador, who licked the blood as if he were licking an ice cream cone. Lucio grabbed the knife, cut off the turtle's head, and tossed it aside, even as its jaws were still snapping. He lifted the turtle's carcass and tipped it over the edge of an improvised bucket, causing a thick stream of blood to pour out.

"We will have to drink it while it is still hot," said Salvador. "It will thicken quickly if we don't." Salvador passed the bucket to Señor Juan, who put up his hand to refuse it. Then he offered it to Farsero, who also declined. Salvador took a swig and gave it to Lucio, who gulped it down like a chocolate milk shake, blood dripping from the corners of his mouth.

"*Vampiro!*" Jesús shouted, laughing at Lucio. "Let me have some." Jesús threw his head back and drank the turtle blood. He was surprised by the sweetness of it. Jesús passed the bucket to Salvador, who again offered it to Señor Juan and Farsero. This time Señor Juan sniffed it, closed his eyes, took a sip, and swallowed. He immediately jumped up and spit it over the side. Then he began to gag, soon vomiting into the water.

Meanwhile, Jesús was ripping the turtle to pieces as the steaming-hot flesh oozed blood. He rinsed the raw meat with seawater and gave it to Salvador, who carved it up like a Thanksgiving turkey. They devoured every bit of it—intestines, fat, and eyeballs. They sucked the jellylike marrow from the bones and scraped the shell clean. Jesús, Lucio, and Salvador enjoyed their meal of raw meat and could not understand why Señor Juan and Farsero would not eat it.

It would be two weeks before they'd find anything else to eat.

Birds, most likely blue-footed or masked boobies, occasionally landed on the edges of the boat and on the bow enclosure. Salvador would sit quietly with his shirt in his hands and wait, like a tiger ready to pounce on its prey. Having had little exposure to humans this far out at sea, the unsuspecting birds were no match for him. In one lightning-quick motion, he could trap a bird in his jacket, snap its neck, and then announce that breakfast would soon be served.

Jesús was so impressed by Salvador's ability that he nicknamed him *"el Gato,"* which means "the cat." After plucking the feathers, Jesús, Salvador, and Lucio would eat everything but the bones, including the duck-like webbing on the bird's feet. Farsero and Señor Juan gagged on the raw bird meat and gave up trying to eat it.

In early December the men noticed that barnacles had formed on the bottom of the boat. The barnacles contained bits of food that attracted turtles and smaller fish. The smaller fish, of course, attracted bigger fish. From this point on, food was plentiful. But there would be little rain through the end of February. So the fishermen drank the blood of sea turtles to stay hydrated.

They sliced off the turtle heads and gulped from the turtles like chalices.

7. Soul Mates

I had been at the television job in Atlanta for about six weeks, and I was ready to make my next big move.

I bought a marquis-shaped diamond engagement ring. Carmen was coming to visit to check out internships, but I had a longer commitment in mind. I shared my plans with some of my coworkers, who seemed nice enough and would eventually become my family in Atlanta. But they were very intense about selling TV advertising. After work one day, one of the guys who had taken me under his wing asked me to go out for drinks.

"This isn't my idea," he said as we were driving to the bar, "but everyone in the office has nominated me to tell you we don't think you should get married. You're too young, and this job is hard on marriages. Long hours. All the entertaining."

But they didn't know Carmen. They didn't really know me. I told him that I knew what I was doing and that they should keep their noses out of my business. Carmen was the best thing that had ever happened to me, and I didn't need them telling me how to live my life. I loved her, and I was going to marry her. End of conversation.

"I've delivered the message," he said, shrugging his shoulders. "Now let's get some cocktails." I assume he went back and told my colleagues that I had rejected their advice. A short time later, though, Carmen came to town, and all the people at the office went out of their way to be gracious to her.

I picked up Carmen at the airport and tried to find the park I had seen on a map. I had a picnic basket in the trunk with some chilled wine and roasted chicken—the whole schmear. I tried to stay cool but was having trouble locating the park, and soon I became angry.

"It's okay," Carmen said. "We can just go back to your apartment."

"No!" I said much louder than I meant to. "This has to be just right." *Very subtle.*

She knew right away. Two hours later I finally found the park and pulled out warm wine, cold chicken, and a jewelry box.

"Will you marry me?"

"Yes."

One point four seconds. Done.

Her mom helped us with everything we had to do for the wedding. Her dad was happy when the bar opened. We got some cool gifts (including a pair of Chuck Taylor high tops and a shoehorn) and went to Mexico for our honeymoon, where I got sick as a dog. We came back to a brand-new condominium with new furniture and two new cars. I had a great job in TV, and Carmen had gotten her dream job—flight attendant.

She was twenty-two, and I was twenty-three, and, well, we didn't have a clue. We both were from a small town, had gone to school in a small town.

We didn't know anything about anything. Most of the men in my family got married right out of high school, so I figured I had really taken my time.

The TV business was fast paced and fun. The people were dynamic and loved to have a good time. It didn't take much to get people to show up for drinks. *It's your birthday? Well, let's have some drinks... You got a promotion? That calls for drinks... You got fired? Drinks... It's Wednesday?... You're pregnant?... Drinks!*

A willing participant in all the fun, I didn't miss a chance for the latest celebration. I remember thinking, *These people have a problem.* Little did I know that I would soon be one of "these people."

I worked two years in that first TV job before another TV company, Tribune Broadcasting, owner of WGN and the Chicago Cubs, offered me double the money to come work for them. I jumped at the opportunity. I loved the Cubs. Two years later the studio offered to double my salary, so I jumped again.

I didn't really have any sense about what was driving me. I had never developed any sort of decision-making skills, because most of my decisions were based on shame and fear. Usually my decisions were to run from something that was painful in my life or to run toward something that gave me validation. In all of it, I was chasing worldly success—the deals, the promotions, and the money—because they gave me a sense of worth.

Carmen loved me and supported my career moves, although she also saw how often I was well intentioned but sorely misguided. She had her own ambitions but shelved them for mine. Unlike me, she didn't really need to have a job to be comfortable with herself, to know her value and significance.

I persuaded Carmen to give up her job, and we headed west. We moved to company headquarters in Los Angeles. We lived in a little bungalow in the valley near the studio.

I was on the road selling the show *227.* When I checked into a hotel in Colorado Springs, the bellman opened the door to my room, and on the bed I saw a little teddy bear with a ribbon attached to two balloons filled with helium—one pink and one blue. *What a cute gift for the guests,* I thought. *Too bad I don't have kids.*

I walked over to the bed and read the card: "We are in the pink…or… the blue. Love, Carmen."

I didn't understand. I turned to the bellman to tip him, and then it registered. I looked back at the note. "Oh my! I'm going to be a father!" I exclaimed to the bellman.

He was not moved. "Where would you like your bag?"

I called Carmen, and we both squealed with joy. Then I headed down to the hotel bar, listened to some ragtime on the player piano, drank beer from a giant flute, and eventually calmed down enough to fall asleep.

We had been in L.A. for about two years and saw that it was nothing like the Middle-America environment we had grown up in and wanted to raise our kids in. When I discovered that every major studio but ours had an office in Dallas, I put together a presentation for my boss to show him why we needed one there too. I was traveling to Dallas every week anyway, so it made perfect sense to live there.

Carmen happened to have a doctor's appointment on the day of my presentation. I got up early, went to the office and rehearsed, then met with my boss.

Carmen called later that morning to tell me she was ready to go to the doctor. I looked at my watch. "Honey, the appointment isn't for another two hours," I said.

"We need to go now."

"In a couple of hours, the traffic won't be so bad," I said.

"I need to go now."

"But—"

"Joe, you need to come home right now!"

"What? Oh boy!… Are you… Is it happening?"

"Just come get me as soon as possible," Carmen said calmly.

I rushed home and found her sitting in the kitchen in the dark with her suitcase next to the back door and our dog, Ginger, the crazy brown-spotted Dalmatian, at her side. Ginger had no idea when we left her that day that when we returned, she would no longer be our baby. She would just be a dog.

"How was your presentation?" Carmen asked.

"What?… Good, I guess… Where's your suitcase?"

"It's right here," she said, pointing at it.

"Should we go straight to the emergency room? Should I call an ambulance?" My head was spinning, and Carmen's contractions were coming regularly, several minutes apart.

"I already talked to the doctor's office," she said. "They said to come there first." She told me her contractions had been fairly steady since 4:00 a.m.

"Why didn't you tell me this morning?" I growled.

"I didn't want to worry you before your presentation," she said.

I had already forgotten about that. (Important marriage note: *Wife in labor trumps presentation.*)

We made the trip to his office near Cedars-Sinai in record time and then got a private labor-and-delivery room that was nicer than our house: hardwood floors, TV with VCR, private bath and shower. The Hollywood sign was visible from our window. In those days insurance paid for the best, and they paid 100 percent. *We could vacation here,* I remember thinking.

Carmen's labor pains came more frequently, and I was coaching her just as they had shown us in Lamaze class. She was determined not to have any drugs and was working hard through each contraction. Then she suddenly stalled out. The doctor told us to walk around the hospital floor to get things going again, so they hooked her up to a portable IV stand, and we left the room.

When we stopped to rest, I stepped into the visitors' lounge and spotted Abe Vigoda. (If you were born before 1970 or watch TV Land, you know him as "Fish.") I qualify on both counts, plus I sold the *Barney Miller* show— 170 episodes' worth. Vigoda was sitting on the sofa, staring at the floor, all alone in the maternity ward at Cedars-Sinai.

Only in L.A.

We had a beautiful baby girl.

And I wasn't the only one who thought so. One day Carmen and our little Pookie came to have lunch in the commissary on the studio lot. We were standing in line to pay when our daughter peeked her little head over Carmen's shoulder. The chairman of the television division slid into line behind us.

"That is the most beautiful baby I have ever seen," he said.

Did you hear that? He said we have the most beautiful baby he has ever seen! It was affirmation of a job well done! I had hit the very high Hollywood standard, no less, of approval for baby production.

Three weeks later the studio said yes to my plan for a Dallas office. My presentation had worked. I jumped at the chance to get out of the line of fire at the studio headquarters, and we were on an airplane that afternoon. We couldn't get out of Los Angeles fast enough.

I was on cloud nine, but for some of the wrong reasons. I had a lovely baby girl, a beautiful wife, a job others would kill for, and all the toys and perks that come with a life of privilege. Life was good, and we were living large.

Outwardly we appeared as though we had made it, but I was just getting started on self-deception. To be sure, I truly loved my wife, and my daughter was my pride and joy. No question. But in another sense they, too, were symbols of success that I included in the virtual picture I wanted to frame and put over the couch and make sure everyone could see. I had so much yet was driven to have more. I wasn't content deep down. And as happy as I was with Carmen and my new daughter, I was also vacant inside because of other things. Other things expected and unrealized.

I kept searching for more. *More of what?* I really didn't know. Something. I couldn't put my finger on it, but it felt like it was out there, just around the corner. Something to fill the emptiness inside me. When I didn't find it the next day or the next week or in the next deal or the next promotion, I learned to fill this emptiness with material things, including a few barrels of single-malt Scotch, which helped dull the inner ache. The long flights in first class were the treatment chamber.

We settled into a nice area of Dallas called Preston Hollow, with tree-lined streets, young families, and plenty of grass for me to cut. We bought a fixer-upper two streets over from the son of President George H. W. Bush, opened an office for the company a few blocks away, and started to fall in love with the great state of Texas.

By living in Dallas, I had shorter flights, but I still consumed the same amount of liquor or even more, just in smaller periods of time. I wondered, *How much longer can I keep this up?*

Carmen got into the business of full-time mommydom, complete with another precious baby girl. She rallied the new neighbors around an old park that needed to be fixed up, while I established the studio's presence in the region. I could make day trips out and back to most of the markets in the area and got to spend more time at home with my girls. I started to get introduced as Carmen's husband and could remain fairly anonymous—outside the microscope of HQ. I even came close to making a few friends of my own.

There was a Catholic campus ministry just across the street on the campus of Southern Methodist University, and we started to attend services regularly.

A young priest there grabbed my attention because during his homilies, I felt as if he were speaking directly to me. It piqued my curiosity, so I signed up for adult education classes and decided to join the Catholic Church. It seemed like a logical step to take. I was even flying back into town just to be part of the class on Tuesday nights. I remember feeling a vague connection to God every now and again. It would come in a moment of looking at one of the kids when she was sleeping or seeing something beautiful in nature (when I would pause for thirty seconds to notice nature), but then I'd brush it off with a *Nah, there is no way that feeling can be a connection to God. Why would He want to have anything to do with me? There's no way I can deserve His attention...*

It was as if checking "going to church" off the list would perhaps get me closer to filling the emptiness inside me. We attended regularly, but when that one priest wasn't there, it wasn't the same. He was moved to Rome, and my interest soon faded. I basically thought, *Hey, I tried it, and it didn't work.* I moved on. I still went to Mass almost every weekend, but it was just checking another thing off the list.

Another career opportunity came along, and we moved back to Atlanta and settled in for the second time. We bought a larger house. I threw in a new Harley-Davidson and a home theater.

My need for approval continued to rear its ugly head, usually when my dad would visit. On one such occasion the two of us were sitting in the living room, not talking, which was our usual mode of communication.

This time he said something out of the blue: "How much do you make?"

I told him that was personal and I'd rather not say.

"How much?" he insisted.

"I really don't know exactly," I said. "It's a lot."

"How much is a lot?"

"I really don't want to talk about this. It's embarrassing."

"How much?"

Here we were, sitting in a very nice house with my Porsche 911 Cabriolet parked in the driveway. My kids were in private school, and we spent money like it grew on one of the trees in our perfectly manicured backyard.

"How much?" he asked again.

"With bonuses, car allowance, profit sharing, and benefits, our income is…" I whispered a number in his ear. It was a very big number.

He paused, then said, "I thought it would be more than that."

It was a dagger through my heart. He invalidated my entire existence in eight words.

What do I have to do to win his approval? I was in my late thirties. I had been more successful than anyone in the history of my family. I had done more, made more, and acquired more than I had ever dreamed possible. But I was still desperate for him to be proud of me. After that incident, all the deals I had made, the money, the promotions, the big houses, the toys—all the distractions I had used to deflect the pain—suddenly stopped working.

What is it all for if he is never going to recognize all the hard work? I felt like a small speck on his horizon.

What would it take for him to actually see…*me*?

8. LIFE AND DEATH

Air, food, and water. The simplest elements of survival. An abundance of each surrounded the five men. But being called "water" doesn't make it drinkable. Being called "food" doesn't mean everyone will eat it. Searching for the right survival elements meant choosing what worked for each man. Some days gave up only enough rain for a sip to wet the tongue.

Jesús and Lucio used what was left of the tools to dismantle the outboard motor. They retrieved several cables, some one-inch steel springs from the carburetor, and a yard-long drive shaft. Lucio twisted the springs into fish hooks and used the cables as fishing line. Salvador worked to make a spear by sharpening one end of the drive shaft on the whetstone, which took him several days. When he got tired and his hands were nearly raw, Lucio would take over. Salvador also broke off a two-foot section of the wooden molding on top of one of the dividers in the boat to make a stake and, using his knife, carved a sharp point on one end. Jesús put the fishing line in the water with no bait.

After two days he had not had a bite.

In early December, Salvador was standing watch, looking for boats, when a small fish swam toward them. He readied his drive-shaft spear, which had a short piece of nylon rope attached to it so he could throw it at a fish and pull it back in. Salvador took a shot with his spear and missed. He thought he had tied the nylon rope tightly, but the spear slid through the knot and disappeared into the darkness of the ocean. He screamed at himself in frustration.

The next day a small fish flew into the belly of the boat. Salvador sliced off five finger-length pieces of it and handed one to each man. Jesús, Lucio, and Salvador gobbled theirs down as if it were a chunk of fine sirloin. Señor Juan tried to swallow his piece, but it came back up, sending him into a fit of heaving that produced bile and blood. He had been getting weaker over the past couple of days. Only a week earlier he had stood up in the boat, flexed his biceps, and declared, "I am strong!"

According to Lucio's watch, it was December 12, the feast day of Our Lady of Guadalupe, the patron saint of the Americas, when another sea turtle approached the boat and Salvador went over the side to capture it. Lucio saw this as a sign that God was still with them. According to tradition, this was a day to reflect on issues of faith and to ask God for greater understanding. The men enjoyed their turtle feast and decided to keep track of the turtles they caught by scratching notches in the boat with a nail. Lucio had removed the engine cover and set it on top of the bow enclosure to use as a stove to dry out and cook meat in the sun. Barnacles continued to form on the bottom of the boat, attracting more fish. Including sharks.

The men used any extra turtle meat they had for bait.

Nearly six weeks had passed since their ordeal began.

Around December 17 another storm blew in that was more violent than the one that had taken the fishing net. The panga was pushed to the top of huge swells and thrown down with incredible force into troughs of foam and darkness. Parts of the engine, the fishing hooks, some of the lines, and the engine cover were lost. In the midst of the frenzy, Señor Juan sat on the side of the boat with his legs hanging over the edge.

"Do you want to die?" Jesús yelled at him.

Señor Juan ignored him.

"You are making the ocean angry!" Jesús said. "Stop it!"

Over the next few days, Señor Juan began to suffer from delusions, and Salvador prayed for him. Farsero mostly sat by himself and cried. Lucio's ears started bleeding from an infection. Señor Juan and Lucio wrapped themselves in blankets and huddled under the bow covering while Salvador prayed and read his Bible. Salvador occasionally attempted to engage the others in reading it as well. For now they had food, hydration from the turtle blood, and water from intermittent rainfall.

By Christmas the fishermen were a thousand miles from San Blas.

Back home, Lucio's grandmother, Panchita, decorated her table and set a place for Lucio. She had set a place for him at dinner ever since he was considered missing. She prayed for his safe return twice a day in front of the picture of the Virgin Mary that served as the focal point of her homemade altar. Every day she would read the Tuesday prayer from her tattered prayer book because the last time she saw Lucio was on a Tuesday:

> O Lord God omnipotent, I beseech Thee by the Precious
> Blood of Thy divine Son Jesus that was shed in His bitter
> crowning with thorns, deliver the souls in purgatory, and
> among them all, particularly that soul which is in the greatest
> need of our prayers, in order that it may not long be delayed

in praising Thee in Thy glory and blessing Thee forever.
Amen.[1]

Against her wishes, some family members organized a memorial service for Lucio, which she refused to attend.

"He is alive," she continued to insist. "I know it. My mother told me in a vision." She swore that her mother, who had died several years earlier, often spoke to her in dreams. "She came to me and told me he is on the sea with other men. I asked her when I could have him back, and she told me, 'Not yet, but soon.'"

Lucio had been bleeding from his ears for eight days. Salvador told him he must pray to God and ask for healing. Exhausted, Lucio finally gave in and began to pray.

Señor Juan was now incoherent most of the time, and Salvador pleaded with him to eat something. "Juanito, you can't survive if you don't eat," he said. "Tell me what you want, and I will catch it and dry it out for you in the sun."

"I have all the best cereals at home," Señor Juan said, staring out at the water.

"We are not at home, Juanito. If you don't eat, you will die."

"I can't do it," said Señor Juan. "It's disgusting, and I will only throw up again." His mood turned somber. "I really messed up, didn't I? I got us all in trouble."

"It's okay," said Salvador. "But you have to eat."

"I'll take two pairs of sandals," Señor Juan shouted to no one in particular. "One pair for me and one pair for my mother." Salvador quietly backed away, leaving his companion alone with his delusions.

Over the next ten days, Señor Juan deteriorated rapidly. Salvador and Jesús tried to make him as comfortable as possible, rinsing his mouth, washing his face, cleaning him. When he wasn't yelling out or muttering bizarre statements, Señor Juan moaned in agony. Finally his eyes rolled back into his skull, and his tongue hung out.

Salvador was fishing when he heard Señor Juan shout. "What is it, *hermano*?" Salvador asked, moving in close. Señor Juan did not answer. The commotion woke Jesús.

"Is he alive?"

"No," Salvador said softly. "He is dead."

Death arrived with no announcement and with no permission. It took Señor Juan and left a reminder that this was no dream and that sometimes the hope of returning home to those you love also dies. Sometimes people walk out the door for the last time. Señor Juan went out for a few days to fish. He never returned.

Jesús started to cry. The prospect of death was now a personal reality to each of the survivors. The men undressed Señor Juan and washed him clean. Hours later the body stiffened with rigor mortis. They decided to keep the body on the boat for a few days in hopes of rescue and a proper burial.

Conditions in the middle of the Pacific can reduce a dead body to bones in nine days, experts say. Without oxygen flowing through the body, tissues and cells break down, releasing fluids and gases that create pressure within the body, causing it to inflate as the fluids move into body cavities. After only a few days, the fluids and gases leak out and the body collapses; the skin develops a creamy consistency, begins to turn black, and smells of decay.

Three days after Señor Juan died, the men were overcome by the smell and had to bury him at sea. Farsero sat by himself crying while the other men lifted the body to the top of the bow enclosure. Salvador placed a rosary around Señor Juan's neck. He said seven prayers before they threw the body overboard. As they did, a piece of skin from the body came off in Lucio's hand. He shuddered and threw it in the water, and they watched the body float away.

9. LOST

The shaming talk and the withholding of affection and approval that were used to control my behavior as a child were now playing out in my life as an adult.

In my job I had positional authority. I had tenure. I had a title. Yet I had to keep working like crazy to maintain everything I had. If I let up, I would be a failure. Words from childhood came back to punish me: "You're not good enough for that"; "You'll probably mess that up too"; "You'll never amount to anything." While it was killing me to keep up the pace of my life, it was impossible for me to slow down. I simply would not tolerate failure from myself.

Ironically, for all that I had, I was powerless.

There was much I didn't know that I didn't know. The person we are closest to—our own self—is the hardest one to see. Denial is powerful, and it keeps us from looking in the mirror. At that time I would never had said that I was lost in life. I didn't know enough about myself to be able to verbalize that. Yet I had a disquieting feeling that I was not capable of continuing the mad life I had created. I sensed that some things inside me were not well and that I was drifting.

If anyone found out about these self-doubts, I believed it would be the beginning of everything toppling down. I needed to maintain the grand illusion. So I continued to sit on the deck chair of the *Titanic* and listen to the music play. I acted as if everything was fine, good, better than ever. And I never told anyone about my doubts, the cracks in my certainty. Not even Carmen.

How could I let anyone know that I was falling apart? What would they think of me? What would Carmen think of me?

Stresses began to take a physical toll. I was experiencing shortness of breath and an increased heart rate. But my doctor believed the cause of these symptoms was not as much physical as psychological. He suggested I might be suffering from generalized anxiety disorder. Whenever I was under pressure, my body released massive amounts of adrenaline, increasing my breathing and heart rate, a classic fight-or-flight response.

The good news, he said, was that it was treatable. The bad news was that I was always under pressure. Anxiety was part of my job description. My industry demanded my performance, no matter what.

I left the doctor's office with a prescription for Xanax in hand. I got it filled right away and took one. It helped, so I took more.

I had to fly to Dallas to complete a deal a colleague had been working on when he suffered a stroke. After a few days I called the doctor to say that I was out of pills and that the dosage was barely taking the edge off.

He was horrified. He had given me a month's supply, enough to get a grieving widow through her husband's funeral and beyond. My prescription couldn't even get me out of Texas.

The pain I had deep down inside of me was real. It was physical pain attached to beatings that no one deserves. It was emotional pain attached to verbal abuse and shaming words used to control. It was all the pain that had never been spoken about. It had never been dealt with.

Actually, I had started medicating myself at a very young age. I used my imagination to escape the harshness of my situation. Once a chemical factor (beer) was introduced, it made my escape much faster and easier. It was almost instantaneous. Eventually I used a physical escape as well. I literally "escaped" the locations that caused me so much pain.

Now here was the discovery of a chemical that intensified the relief from the pain. It left no hangover and was prescribed by a licensed professional. It was like winning the lotto!

But where would it end?

Around that time I went to Iowa to connect with my college friend Pee-Wee for a weekend of golf. Out on the course he casually told me that a couple of months earlier he had become so depressed that he'd considered buying a pistol at a pawnshop. He said he was now taking Prozac, and it was helping. This guy was one of the happiest, most entertaining guys on the face of the earth. And he was on Prozac? It sounded like a bad joke.

In the Crown Room at the airport before I boarded my plane back to Atlanta, I surfed the Web for information about depression. One site offered a ten-question quiz. I answered yes to every one.

At the risk of sounding like one of those needy, self-diagnosing guys with too much time on his hands, I broached the subject with my doctor when I got home. I told him about my friend and how I had aced the depression quiz. He took that seriously, prescribing an antidepressant to go with the anxiety medication.

It became a rough year.

Depression was getting the better of me, and anxiety was munching on the leftovers. In time I tried a long list of antidepressants: Celexa, BuSpar, Effexor, Zoloft, Paxil, Lexapro, Wellbutrin, and trazodone. As if walking around sweaty, shaky, and paranoid weren't enough, I had dry mouth, diarrhea, insomnia—almost every side effect the fast-talking voice-over squeezes into the end of prescription drug commercials on TV.

On my next visit to the doctor, I tossed out an idea.

"I think I need to stop drinking," I said.

"What makes you say that?"

"Well, I've been noticing that whenever I drink alcohol with my medication, I fall down a lot."

My feeble attempt at humor failed to convince my doctor—or me—that I was okay. Fact was, on a typical Saturday I would get up, pop open a beer around ten o'clock, and keep on drinking until I went to bed.

We agreed that I should cut back, and I left with a prescription to counter the effects of alcohol just in case I couldn't stop on my own, which it turned out I couldn't. (Quitting turned out to be a lot harder than just deciding to quit.) My doctor also put me in touch with a local psychiatrist who recommended a twelve-step program. My life was becoming a made-for-TV movie. I agreed to go.

For a while I just sat back and listened as the meetings became another buoy that kept me afloat. I did ninety AA meetings in ninety days. I haven't had a drop since.

At the time, giving up alcohol seemed like the answer to all my problems.

Life at the studio got worse. Professionally, I was in a downward spiral, and no matter how hard I tried, I couldn't pull out of it. After fourteen years on the job, I was being treated like an intern, and I began to retreat and get defensive.

I could not perform well. People noticed. It seemed as if everyone was waiting for me to screw up big. I was humiliated but defiant, despite the advice I had been given to lie low and wait out the storm. Some people were probably trying to help me out of the fog, but if so, I didn't notice them.

A few months later I was summarily dismissed. It had taken almost fifteen years to climb up that ladder and a millisecond to fall off.

Strangely, I felt relieved. At least I didn't have to pretend anymore. I made plans to take some time off, but before I could really get my feet up, a friend called with an idea that piqued my interest. He had a business associate who had founded an Internet company in the late nineties and was both a billionaire and a great guy. He owned an interest in a little company called HowStuffWorks, an online encyclopedia of sorts. He envisioned a television show based on this concept, with an edgy entertainment angle, and my friend thought I was the guy to make it happen.

Without giving it much thought, I hopped on board in early spring 2002 and was eventually asked to run the company, which was losing money at the time. I flew up to their headquarters in Cary, North Carolina, every week and continued to go to AA meetings. Things were okay but not great. It was good to have the meds. They were helping.

I had quit drinking, but I started smoking and got hooked right away. I was able to help move HowStuffWorks from losing money to breaking even, though I knew it probably would have happened anyway because they had great content.

I had been there about two years when I started to stall, and so did the company. I couldn't focus again, couldn't remember things. My anxiety came back with a vengeance, and so did the depression.

My doctor upped the dosage on both medications, which seemed to be all I had to fight with.

Near Christmas of that year, I was having lunch with some friends when I got a call from Carmen. The security company that monitored our house had just called her. Something had set off the smoke alarm in the garage, and the fire department had been dispatched. I shrugged it off and told her to call me back if there was a real fire.

There was, and she did.

As I turned onto my street, I saw several fire trucks in front of the house and plumes of black smoke billowing from the second-story windows. Some of the firefighters were reeling in the hoses; they had already put out the flames. Carmen was standing on the front lawn, talking to the battalion chief about what might have caused the fire. Apparently, our housekeeper had dumped the fireplace ashes into a trash can in the garage, unaware that the embers were still hot. The entire garage and attic above were destroyed.

I listened intently to the fireman for a few minutes, looked at the mess in front of me, and…decided to mow the lawn.

Now, I'm not sure why I did that. A wise man once told me that the reason some men love to cut grass is that it requires little brainpower and gives a sense of instant accomplishment. You simply put the wheel on the line where you just mowed, and go. When you're done, you can sit on the porch, crack open a beer, and admire your work. With nobody yelling at you. It's virtually idiotproof. Maybe that was it. My life was out of control, my house was smoldering, and I was powerless. The one thing I could do was mow. I could control and overpower the grass.

With our house uninhabitable, I insisted that we check into the Ritz-Carlton to spend the holidays. Carmen went about the postfire cleanup, and I acted as if nothing were amiss. I was no help to her because, frankly, I liked living at the Ritz. It was a luxurious way to suspend reality, a life-size Xanax complete with room service and cozy European-style down duvets.

Despite the plush accommodations, I needed more to fight off reality.

I took whatever pills I could get my hands on and grew darker with each passing day.

A few weeks later I decided to make a trip to south Texas to visit my dad, a trip that in my imagination held the promise of change, possibly even a breakthrough. I told him I was coming to play golf and get some sun. But I went because I wanted answers. Was my depression hereditary? I had once heard my dad mention something about being depressed. How big a deal was that? Was it something that all the men in the family wrestled with? I needed to know. I was desperate.

I headed to Brownsville, where my father spent a few months each winter. The first night we went across the border to have dinner in Mexico. After we finished eating, I took a breath, confessed to my father that I was suffering from depression, and asked him how he had been able to deal with it so long ago.

"I've never had a problem with any of that," he said, looking me straight in the eye. "I turned forty once too. You'll get over it."

I couldn't believe what I had just heard. This wasn't about turning forty. How could my own father trivialize my pain and desperation? I couldn't believe he refused to admit what I knew he had said years earlier. I couldn't believe my dad would lie to me.

Most of all, I couldn't believe I had expected my father to be any different from what he had always been. But it still hurt.

I walked across the street to a little gift shop with a flashing *"Farmacia"* sign in the window. I was ready to kill the pain even if it killed me in the process. I bought as much as they would sell me: Vicodin, Valium, and more Xanax. I spent the rest of the weekend buying drugs in buckets, taking as much as I could and stuffing the rest in my golf bag. Out of my mind on prescription meds on the way home, I missed my connecting flight in Houston. Blocks of time were disappearing.

Back in Atlanta, the downward spiral continued. The pills had become like alcohol to me, only worse. But I didn't feel as guilty because I thought of them as part of my medical treatment. I took pills in the morning, and by the time I got to work, I was ready for another round. By dinnertime I was ready for more pills and the dark comfort of my bed. I would sleep fourteen hours, then start the process all over the next morning.

I was one of the walking dead.

10. Choosing Life

Farsero cried for days after Señor Juan's funeral.

He had come on this trip as a friend of Señor Juan's. He shared nothing with the others and spoke only to his friend. He frequently said, "I'm El Farsero. That is all you need to know," and with that no one would say or ask anything more. His self-imposed isolation just added to his mystery. Perhaps he was escaping a life in some other place. Or perhaps he was simply shy. Either way, he couldn't have imagined that it would turn out like this. He didn't offer to help, nor did he ask for any.

His despondency became depression, which became relinquishment. He no longer cared about himself. He wouldn't crawl under the bow cover to get out of the sun. His skin bubbled and peeled.

Then at some point he stopped crying. The silence mirrored his life. He was someone's son, but who knew him? He was someone's friend, but who knew his dreams and hopes? No one.

One morning Farsero didn't wake up.

"That is the best death to have," Lucio said: "To die while you are dreaming."

Just as they had done for Señor Juan, they kept Farsero's body on board for three days, praying that a ship would come so he could have a decent burial. Finally the stench became unbearable. Farsero's service was similar to Señor Juan's, except that this time each of the men read a passage from the Bible.

That night Salvador secretly offered God a simple deal: "Dear God," he prayed, "I will give my life if You will allow my friends to live. Amen."

In mid-February it started to rain heavily. Once the gas containers were full, each of the men was able to take a bath in the rainwater that collected in the bottom of the panga. They had not eaten for two weeks, even though the waters were full of food-sharks circling the boat. None of the men wanted to risk becoming a tiger shark's next meal. The sharks were small but ferocious enough to easily bite off an arm.

Late one afternoon Salvador and Jesús saw a five-foot shark just off the side of the boat. Salvador grabbed the wooden stake and plunged it into the head of the shark from the front. The angle of the impalement prevented the shark from diving or pulling away to free itself.

"Hold this and don't let it get away!" Salvador shouted to Jesús, handing him the stake. Salvador stood up and ripped off his shirt. "The knife!" he yelled to Lucio, motioning to the tools. Lucio gave a shark knife to Salvador, who bit down on it and jumped into the bloody water. He grabbed the shark with both hands, one on each side fin, while the shark thrashed violently back and forth. Salvador slowly gained control of the shark, turning it as if he were steering a jet ski, trying to wear the shark down. Jesús hung on to the side of the boat and gained some leverage to jam the stake deeper into the hard muscle of the shark's head. Salvador steadied the animal and was preparing to let go of the right fin and take the knife out of his mouth when the shark thrashed wildly. Having released the fin to grab the knife, Salvador was losing the battle and tiring quickly as he tried to keep his head above the surface of the foam and blood.

"More sharks!" Lucio screamed when he spotted several tigers approaching rapidly.

Salvador's head was under the murky water, so he could not hear the warning or see anything. He kicked his legs and lifted his head toward the fin, locking his teeth on it and biting down as hard as he could. Instantly, he felt a burning pain in his mouth from the tiny thornlike denticles that covered the shark's fin. He raised the knife over his head and with all his strength tried to drive it into the side of the shark, but the blade bounced off as if it had hit solid steel. Salvador raised the knife again, this time plunging it into the shark's eye. The tiger went limp. Lucio and Jesús lifted the shark into the boat and then pulled Salvador out of the water. The shark was still snapping its jaws when Lucio grabbed the knife and twisted it deeper into the creature's brain.

Salvador's lip was split, and two of his teeth were loose. His chest was badly scratched and bleeding. But he was smiling.

Today was his birthday.

The three men devoured the shark—brain, eyes, and stomach, including all its contents. Lucio and Jesús reserved the heart and liver for Salvador and insisted he take them. When the men had finished eating, they sliced the remaining meat into steaks, rinsed them in salt water, and laid them out on the bow to dry.

In March the rain came almost every day. Turtles and birds were plentiful, and there was a seemingly endless supply of fish. Thanks to their protein-rich diet, their need to hang off the back of the boat and discharge their solid waste now occurred only every other week.

By April they were nearing the Pacific shipping lanes and counted more than a dozen large vessels in the distance, still too far off to see the panga. Lucio kept track by cutting notches in the side of the boat.

They invented games to pass the time, one of which was "What Will You Have for Dinner?" They would imagine that the meat they were eating was a piece of hot bread or a favorite fruit, vegetable, or dessert.

"A cheeseburger and a Coke," Salvador would often say, "with chocolate cake and vanilla ice cream."

Lucio's favorite was banana bread. "Can you remember how it smells when it's fresh?" Jesús would ask him.

"I can smell cigarettes and pancakes!" shouted Lucio one day. "Just like they are here in the boat!"

Jesús often thought about Jocelyn and little Juanchillo back home and wondered why this was happening to him. He had not been the best of husbands. He knew he had often been cruel to Jocelyn, treating her more like a servant than a wife. Just before he left for San Blas, he had searched in vain for some money he had hidden away. He had yelled at Jocelyn for moving things around. He later found the money in the pocket of his pants but did not apologize. He frequently made her get out of bed when he came home after a night of drinking with his pals, demanding that she make him something to eat.

Now he saw himself for what he had been. Jocelyn was only sixteen when she got pregnant and barely twenty now. He knew she was at home with no money and no idea of what had happened to him. He pictured her working herself to exhaustion trying to raise their son alone. He vowed to God that if he survived this ordeal, he would be a better husband and father. He also vowed to quit drinking. He knew that Jocelyn would be giving birth any day now, and the thought of it brought him to tears.

"Crybaby!" teased Lucio, who was in a dour mood himself. "Are you not a man?"

"I am a man!" Jesús shot back. "But men cry too. I cry because of my family. You don't cry because you have no one."

"I was born just as you," said Lucio. "I have my mother, my father, my grandmother!"

"No," Jesús insisted. "You have no one!"

Salvador had had enough.

"Calm down!" he shouted. "Don't be stupid. We need each other." He ordered them to different parts of the boat, where they remained silent until Lucio finally spoke.

"I'm sorry, Jesús. I shouldn't have said those things to you. It's just the hopelessness."

"God will look after us," Salvador assured them. "He will protect us. We have food and water, and we are friends. God wants us to be friends."

Jesús and Lucio rarely argued after that. From time to time, Lucio trimmed the other men's hair and beards with a shark knife.

On cold nights they would sleep three in a row under the bow enclosure to keep warm. Lying together in close quarters, they would speculate on where they were and where they might end up. Jesús thought Hawaii; Salvador thought China. Lucio had no opinion. Whenever an airplane passed overhead, they would try to guess where it was going. Salvador knew they could not get back to where they had started because of the currents.

Wherever they were headed, he said, they should try to get there faster.

So they went to work fashioning a mast out of the wooden trim on two of the dividers and hoisted a pair of blankets as sails. This did not increase their speed much, but the activity gave them a feeling of accomplishment, and they felt a bit more in control. Soon after, a storm took the sails and nearly capsized the boat.

Through May and June they stuck with the routine: fish, sleep, eat. Although the men didn't know it, during that time the panga passed by several islands—Christmas, Fanning, and Baker—but never near enough for any-one to see them.

By July, the fishermen were facing greater challenges than the heat: Jesús was having severe stomach pains, and Lucio's vision was failing, as was Salvador's. Their energy levels were dangerously low, and they were moving much more slowly. The end was near, and they knew it.

"I do not fear death," Salvador told his companions. "Not when I am with you."

11. Choosing Death

Shortly after my visit with my dad, Carmen and I went to dinner with our friends Howard and Mary.

Back in my drinking days, Howard and I had become good friends. We did guy stuff together: playing golf and tennis, smoking cigars, attending sporting events, going to movies our wives wouldn't go see, and, of course, cocktailing. Back then, I never noticed he was having only one drink to my ten.

I remember once playing golf with him, and I was egging him on. "You should drink more," I blurted out after I hit a long four iron two feet from the flagstick. (I always thought I played better when I was a little tipsy.)

"I am perfectly fine with the amount I drink," he said.

What an odd thing to say, I thought. I couldn't imagine a guy not indulging to the fullest. At the same time, I'm sure I was suppressing an inner voice that was telling me, *Hey, idiot, you should take a lesson from this guy. He has his life together.*

Of course, later I had given up drinking. So when Howard and I next played golf, I was able to tell him, all too proudly, that I hadn't had a drink in forty-three days.

I didn't mention all the pills I was taking.

Several times during the dinner, I got up to use the rest room, and Howard had to keep me from falling down. It was so uncomfortable for Carmen. And so sad. No one knew what to do or say. I, of course, was oblivious.

The next morning Howard asked me to join him for tennis, and I took great pains to sufficiently medicate so I wouldn't feel the weight of his judgment, or anything else for that matter. After I had missed most of the balls he hit to me, he was fed up. We left the court, walked over to the pond, and sat down. He had never looked so serious with me.

In my mind we were "guy" friends, and guy friends usually don't want to mess things up by getting serious. A guy friend usually sits back and watches his buddy implode: "It's none of my business... He's just going through a hard time... He'll find his own way out of it." Not Howard. He wasn't about to show up at my funeral and kick himself for not doing something before it was too late.

"Joe, you have to get help. You're not the same Joe we used to know. You need to go someplace and check out whatever is messing you up."

"Okay," I said. "Okay."

Carmen had been saying the same thing for years, but for some reason I couldn't hear it from her. When Carmen reflected back to me the truth of who I was, I vigorously rejected it. I had a built-in Star Wars missile defense system and was slapping down incoming Soviet truth scuds. She was trying to tell me what she saw, not in an underhanded way to bring me down, but out of love. But back then, I didn't know what I didn't know.

I could hear it from Howard for two reasons. First, I trusted him. Not that I didn't trust Carmen, but other factors cloud the clarity in marriage relationships. Second, I wasn't married to Howard or in business with him.

He had nothing to gain from telling me this. He only had something to lose—our friendship. But he loved me enough to tell me the truth. That much got through to me. He served as an objective third party, who risked his friendship with me for my benefit.

I told Howard I would get help—soon.

But first I had to get through a breakfast meeting with some investors who wanted me to be part of their latest project. The next morning they were waiting expectantly at the Ritz-Carlton for the guy who had been described as "the perfect fit," the guy who "had it all together."

That guy never showed up. But *I* did.

I pulled into the valet line having taken several Xanax tablets and a couple of Vicodin pills from my new Mexican stockpile, just to make sure. I had also elected to double down on a new anxiety drug my doctor thought might help. Suffice it to say that I was in rarer form than usual. I got out of my Porsche, handed the keys to the valet, and walked in, completely out of my mind and certainly not ready for prime time. When I sat down, I started to feel the cumulative effects of the pills. I could feel panic coming on, but the great thing is that as soon as you feel a twinge of anxiety, you take another Xanax, and the anxiety gets whisked away. For me the Xanax was a yummy cream puff. No matter how intense the situation, I felt as if everything was just peachy.

So I thought I could handle it. With pharmaceuticals on my side, I was ready to take command, to be the executive I once was. But this time the Xanax sent me over the top—put me under the table, actually. By the time I ordered my fruit plate, I was slurring, bobbing, and occasionally nodding off.

Still, the yummy Xanax cream puff did its job. It made me think I had pulled it off without a hitch.

When I got home, I doubled over and began a thirty-six-hour cycle of vomiting and diarrhea. On top of everything else, I had gotten the flu. I was the "sickness" part of the "in sickness and in health" vow made flesh, and

Carmen was forced to contend with sights and smells no human being should ever have to deal with or clean up after.

When it was finally over, I experienced one moment of terrible, crystal clarity. I couldn't remember a lot of what had happened, but at least for a moment I was sober enough to see through the fog. I was empty.

Carmen found the stash of medications I had bought in Mexico and confronted me. *Busted.* She called my psychiatrist and told him what was going on. I then took the phone and told him, in a burst of bravery, that I was quitting the antidepressants and anxiety meds cold turkey.

It seemed to me that after years of taking these medications, it wasn't working. Nothing had really made that much of a difference, and if anything, I was worse off than I had ever been. The depression had won the first eleven rounds of a twelve-round fight. I needed to do something drastic.

He advised me not to do it, but I didn't care. I couldn't live like that any longer. If it took pills to keep me going, then I would just as soon die. He insisted that I see him the next day.

I went in and told him I needed the treatment for those at the end of their ropes. The pills weren't working; the sessions weren't working. I needed the serious stuff, and I had to have it right then.

I had spent the previous night researching psychiatric treatment facilities. There were some out west that promised good results. What's more, they offered resort-style accommodations, spa treatments, and beautiful scenery—a Ritz-Carlton for the depressed. It sounded awesome. After all, I didn't want to be with the regular depressed people; I had "designer depression." Beating it was going to take intensive inpatient therapy, four-hundred-thread-count sheets, and an on-call massage therapist.

My doctor, however, thought that spending fifty thousand dollars a month in Arizona didn't make sense when there were programs just as good in Atlanta. He recommended a local outpatient program.

Fine. At least I would be able to sleep in my own bed and spend time with my family. He booked an appointment for me for the next Monday.

As soon as I left his office, I started to worry about the possible ramifications: Was this going to get me fired? What would our friends think? What about my stock options? Surely my boss and the rest of the folks at work would think badly of me and want me out.

On the way home, I took inventory of the what-ifs. I decided I was probably going to get canned. Almost in tears I called my attorney, who told me how I should approach my colleagues, and—if I needed to down the road—how to file a disability claim. Next, I called my closest friends to tell them I was checking into a hospital for depression. Every one of these conversations started and ended in tears. I had never been so publicly humiliated. I had to explain that the guy who was so driven for success had failed. I was no longer capable of figuring things out on my own.

I wasn't going to be the guy with the success story. I was never going to be the son who lived up to his father's expectations. I was never going to be good enough. I was going to lose everything: my family, my job, my reputation—everything. The vow I had taken, against the pain and the wounds of my childhood, to be successful was going to be broken. It was over. I had failed at life.

I was broken.

I spent the rest of the week prepping for my treatment. There were many details to consider, the last of which included calling my office. I started with my boss but couldn't track him down, trading urgent messages and e-mails with his secretary until I got him at his beach house in Miami. I was very nervous, expecting to hear something like, "We can't help you. We can't give you the time off. This is your problem. Don't let the door hit you on the way out."

Instead, he met me with grace and understanding, this billionaire on Fisher Island who, without giving it a second thought, could have easily spent ten times my net worth finding a replacement. "You do whatever you need to do and take whatever time you need to get yourself well," he said. "We'll take care of everything around here until you get back."

I hung up the phone and cried.

The next morning I woke up with the familiar pain, fear, and uneasiness.

Around ten I got a call from Joshua, a friend with whom I shared interests in a number of things, particularly football. As the drama coach at my kids' school, Joshua kept a watch on my babies and reported back to me if we needed to institute any "double secret probations." His kids were *really* babies, and Carmen and I fell in love with them as if they were our grandchildren. He and his wife, Allison, are fifteen years younger than we are, so we took them under our wings, and they became as close as a brother and sister.

That day Carmen and Allison were having a garage sale, and the artifacts from my studio days were going like hot cakes. It was raining, and I was sitting in a lawn chair, tearing up as I watched *Seinfeld* T-shirts, hats, and other memorabilia go for next to nothing—trophies from days gone by, proof that I once had been capable of better things.

Joshua came and drove me to a restaurant, opting for a table in the back. Our iced teas came, and he threw his Bible on the table. He didn't say anything for a while; he just listened to me talk about my fears concerning the psychiatric hospital. After ten minutes, this angel in disguise leaned in close.

"Look," he said. "I'm sure the doctors will have all kinds of great stuff to tell you about why you're depressed. I'm sure you probably have some sort of chemical imbalance." He shifted in his seat before going on. "I don't want you to go into this thinking that some psychobabble and some drugs are going to fix you for good. There's only one lasting solution for your problem, and that is a relationship with God."

I had been to church before. I went to Mass with Carmen and the girls and even taught some Sunday school, and God was all over the AA twelve-step programs I had been attending for the last few years. But I didn't know anything about a relationship with God, and I didn't understand what that had to do with my addiction and depression. Still, I agreed to pray with Joshua right there at the table.

Then an amazing thing happened. The prayer was unlike any other I had ever heard or pretended to pray. It was like one of those southern Bible Belt, "come to Jesus" prayers, the kind where you call out for God's help, knowing full well that if He doesn't show up, you're doomed.

It was a call from deep within another man's heart, with as much power and intensity as a human can convey, to lift me out of my hopelessness and into the hands of an amazing God, who has an endless supply of grace and mercy. Joshua's summons to God had to be strong enough to take my heart along with his as he handed it off to the One who heals.

I had never met Jesus—probably wouldn't have recognized Him if I'd seen Him—but praying this way felt natural and real. I was flinging my heart out over iced tea. When we finished praying, we were both in tears.

That night I crawled under the covers, hoping my iced-tea prayer would take.

When I woke up the next morning, I was terrified. I had quit the painkillers cold turkey. And for the first time in a long time, I felt it all: the emotional anguish, the throbbing grief, the physical pain.

This is where the illusion of success had gotten me. All of that drive toward the illusion was useless. It was a mirage filled with empty promises to quench my thirst. The drive toward success—caused by factors we don't even know about—never ends and never fills. Yet I believed for so long that it somehow could and would.

Everywhere in my life there was doom and dread. It felt as if someone had sucker-punched me in the stomach, then delivered the worst possible news a person could hear: you've been fired, you're going to jail, your wife is leaving you, and your daughter has been kidnapped by a child molester. And, by the way, the IRS is holding for you on line one.

Truthfully, I was hoping for something more—a dramatic, made-for-TV moment, especially considering Joshua's prayer the day before. As the toxins started leaving my body and I was thinking more clearly, I began to wonder if change would ever come. After forty-two years of trying to save myself, what was one prayer going to do? How I wished there was hope in a God who could rescue me, even if it was just from the pain of living. I had tried every other option.

Joshua had almost challenged God during our prayer together. In essence, he said, "God, if You don't come right now to this man, he is going to die." And I believed him.

That Saturday, February 14, was cold, and I was moving slowly. I don't remember a lot, except that I never really got dressed. I put on sweatpants and bedroom slippers and my bomber jacket with the *Seinfeld* logo on the back, because as long as you've got a cool jacket, you're not a loser, right? Carmen was still working the garage sale, and I showed up looking as though I had just escaped from a psych ward. *Happy Valentine's Day, honey! Say, would you mind doing me a favor this year and dropping me off at the loony bin?*

I parked myself in a lawn chair in the rain and tried not to cry. Allison sometimes reminds me how pitiful, afraid, and sad I looked and how she and Joshua prayed that I could hang on for one more day. Carmen was praying too, and she must have been scared to death. Allison stared at me in that lawn chair for the longest time, trying to will me back to wholeness. I didn't even notice.

I felt as if there was no more life left in me, as if there was nothing I could do except wait for the next horrible blow. I had never felt more helpless and alone.

Inside, I cried out, *How did this happen? How did it come to this?*

There was no answer.

12. RESCUE

Jesús, Salvador, and Lucio drifted in the western Pacific roughly six thousand miles from where they had started 286 days earlier.

They were among the Marshall Islands off the coast of Australia, though never in sight of land. They had killed and eaten 108 sea turtles and had seen twenty-five ships during the more than nine months adrift. Two crew members were dead, and Lucio was near death himself. As they huddled together like sardines under the bow enclosure, Salvador felt a thump on the side of the boat. Sharks and whales had thumped the boat on many occasions, but this thump was different.

He also noticed a humming noise.

"Is that the wind?" asked Lucio.

Salvador pulled himself up using the side of the boat and covered his eyes as he squinted into the afternoon sun. He thought he was seeing a mirage.

"Jesús! Lucio!" he shouted. "We are saved!"

"Leave us alone," moaned Lucio. "Let us sleep."

"No, look!" Salvador yelled, pointing. Jesús and Lucio crawled from under the bow enclosure and saw several Asian men pulling alongside them in a small boat, with a gigantic trawler as a backdrop. Registered in Taiwan, the *Koos 102* is more than half the size of a football field, with a predominantly Chinese crew.

The three men were feeble and thirsty. Muscles had atrophied, and their weakness was amplified. Lucio could barely see. They sluggishly pulled themselves out of the bow enclosure and helped each other gain equilibrium while pulling themselves up by the edge of the panga. As each of them peeked over the side of the boat, their eyes met the most beautiful sight they had ever seen. Even though his vision was blurred, Lucio could feel the exhilaration coming from Jesús as he repeated, "Thank You, God. Thank You, God."

Salvador looked to heaven and shook his head in confirmation to "God above us."

Crying and laughing, they were helped into the small rescue boat and then delivered to the trawler. They tried to take it all in, but it was difficult to see anything clearly after so many months of the water reflecting UV rays into their eyes. They were so overcome they didn't even notice the voices of their saviors.

The fishing crew of the enormous craft proceeded as if picking up three men stranded on the ocean was a common experience, as if some sort of modus operandi existed for this situation. In fact, it was fairly common. Small fishing boats were often stranded in the waters around these islands because of engine failure or running short on fuel.

So the crew made quick work of the rescue, hoisting the panga on board. The rescuers seemed more concerned about the panga than the survivors, who huddled together in one spot and continued to cry and to laugh.

A massive fishing vessel like the *Koos* couldn't stop working just because some local fishermen sheared a gear in their outboard. The *Koos 102* had picked up the fishermen on its way out to sea on a tuna-fishing expedition, and that was the crew's first order of business. This meant the fishermen would be at sea for several more weeks until the cargo hold was full.

The crew of the trawler didn't know at the time that these fishermen weren't local, nor did they understand the extraordinary international story they were now a part of.

The crew told the fishermen to stay indoors in an air-conditioned cabin. It was obvious they had been in the sun too long and needed rest and fluids.

The three were restless during their first few nights aboard the ship, tormented by nightmares and the fear that their rescue was just a dream. Many days passed before they could accept the reality that they were safe.

After several days they were summoned to the captain's quarters to meet Yeng Ching Shui, who did not speak Spanish. The fishermen, of course, did not speak Chinese. The captain pointed to a map of the area islands, attempting to learn which one the men had come from. The men were confused. They had never seen these islands on a map before. The fishermen kept shaking their heads no. They realized they somehow had to explain to the captain that they were not from the local islands. They kept stepping back from the map and repeating, "Mexico." Finally, after five attempts, the captain got it. He shook his head as if to say, "Impossible."

The trawler continued to operate as usual with the three guests aboard, staying at sea for two more weeks. Once communications were established with the mainland, the lines started buzzing between the ship, the port, the Mexican authorities, the families of the men, and the owner of the fishing company, who ordered the ship back to Majuro, the capital of the Marshall Islands. When the manager of the port was asked how the fishermen looked when he met them, he said, "A little skinny and exhausted—and understandably so. By the time I saw them on the docks, they were in pretty good condition, but that was two weeks later."

Aboard the *Koos 102,* Jesús, Salvador, and Lucio gained strength each day, gradually adding more substantial food to their diet. They slept well and enjoyed long showers, trying their best to wash away nine months at sea. Their bodies were healing. Lucio regained normal eyesight, and his ears cleared up. They trimmed their hair and nails.

And they continued to read the Bible.

Initially they were fed only rice and fresh water. (Later, when processed foods containing preservatives were added to their diet, the three fishermen got sick, and their limbs began to swell.)

The first time they sat down with the crew in the dining area, after consuming nothing but raw fish, raw turtle meat, and turtle blood for nine months, they were served a special meal: sushi. As the plates were set in front of them, the survivors looked at each other in disbelief.

"They *are* going to cook this, aren't they?" Jesús whispered to Salvador.

"I don't think so."

"What should we do?" asked Jesús through clenched teeth.

"Smile and eat," said Salvador.

13. FOUND

I remember only three things about Sunday, February 15, 2004. The first is kneeling in church, reading the prayer on the back of the missal and questioning why God would allow me to live if this was what my life was going to be—one filled with never-ending fear and doom.

The second is looking at the clock around six that evening, knowing I had an appointment at the Cuckoo's Nest the next morning. And I really didn't care. I was done. Toast. Finished with life.

The last thing is wishing (or hoping) as I crawled into bed, *Please just let me die.*

I had a rude awakening just after midnight, as though someone were holding smelling salts close to my nose, trying to jolt me back into consciousness. I didn't know where I was for a moment. My clothes were drenched. It was as if I had jumped into a pond and forgotten to change before going to bed. I lay there a few minutes, wondering what was going on. Somehow I felt different. I got up and changed into dry clothes and got back into bed. I closed my eyes and breathed in deeply.

Then it came.

Amid all my darkness and failure and uncertainty, I felt the most amazing sense of peace sweeping over me. It was light taking over the dark. I know what this sounds like, and at previous times in my life, I would not have believed others describing something similar. But all I can say is that it was *true,* an experience like none other I'd ever had. It came as a trickle at first, then a rush, as if my heart was a bucket and hope was being poured into it. It filled me deep into my being, and I felt it, physically, all the way down in my feet, then climbing up my body to my knees, my chest, and the top of my head. It flowed into me as if I were a withering plant starving for water, a pure joy flooding my entire body until there was no more room left in me.

It was real. Real joy. Not that whiskey-and-sports-car kind of desperate, giddy pleasure, but a just-got-a-second-chance-at-life kind of deep joy. I had no concern that it would wear off, nor could I do anything to make it stay. The pain was a distant memory. Every ounce of it. The knot in my neck and shoulders, gone; the burning in the pit of my twisted-up stomach, gone; the lump in my throat, gone. I couldn't believe it. The fear and doom and pain had vanished.

I woke up Carmen. "Honey, something has happened."

"What? What is it?" she said, barely awake.

"I think...God has just come into my life," I said, not knowing exactly what I meant by this.

"What are you talking about?" she muttered, still half-asleep.

"I don't know," I said, "but everything is gone. All the pain, all my anxiety—gone."

I could tell she wasn't sure what to make of this. *What drug is he on now?* she must've been thinking.

"I'm okay," I said. "Really. I'm really okay. Somehow I just know everything is going to be okay. I have this amazing peace. A joy. Like I have never felt before. Everything is suddenly calm and serene."

"What do you think it is?" she asked, not really expecting that I had an answer.

"I have no idea," I said. "That's why I woke you up. I thought you'd know."

We sat quietly in bed for a few minutes. I wasn't sure what to say. I'm not usually one to hold back, but I didn't want to freak out Carmen more than I already had. The last thing I needed was to lose my best cheerleader because she thought I had really, *really* gone off the deep end this time.

I was, in a way, afraid to be hopeful. But I knew I had somehow just been rescued. On the eve of my admission to a psychiatric hospital and after years of wrong turns and putting my ladder against the wrong walls, God had shown up on a double dare and done the unthinkable: He had rescued me.

I didn't fully understand exactly what happened that night. Even today, I don't know the mystery of it, but here's what I think: In the simplest of terms, when I formed the thought, *Please just let me die,* I was giving up my tight, desperate hold on my life. I had surrendered the life I had been barely living, not in exchange for another kind of life, but just because I was simply out of options. That night I was free-falling like a jet fighter in a death spiral...and God stretched out His big supernatural safety net and caught me.

For me, surrender was my dying breath, a whisper barely audible. Yet to God it apparently sounded loud and clear, a 911 call for help: "I give up!"

It was me finally giving up my junk and the dream of self-sufficiency.

It was me letting go of the self-delusion that if I earned enough, drank enough, and spent enough, I would "be enough."

It was me saying to my dad, "I won't ever be good enough for you. And, you know, that's okay, because I'm good enough for God."

When I let go of my stuff that night, it had claw marks all over it, because I had clung to it like a lovesick teenager. It was my god. Robert Downey Jr., the actor, once described his stuff to a judge before being jailed for again violating the terms of his parole: "It's like I've got a shotgun in my mouth, with my finger on the trigger, and I like the taste of gun metal." *Brother, I know how you feel.*

Here's the thing. What happened that night was about my relinquishing my tight hold on a fundamental fantasy: the notion that my achievements actually meant something.

The next morning I was still weak, not just from being sick, but because I had been subsisting for weeks on the Diet-Coke-and-Marlboro Happy Meal.

As I stood in front of the mirror, the veil lifted, and for the first time I could see clearly the physical toll my lifestyle had taken on me. I had gone from a borderline handsome guy to a borderline homeless guy. I could see what had been obvious to others for so long. I looked like the disheveled person in the antidepressant TV ads, full of pain and misery. (Those depictions are accurate too. That's how it feels.)

Even though I had been suffering horribly on the inside and it was showing up on the outside, I had deluded myself into thinking I still had game, with my fancy car, my alleged good looks, and my pharmaceuticals. That day, the truth stared me in the face. And it was ugly.

In fact, Carmen had taken the car keys away from me before I had the chance to kill some unsuspecting stranger or myself. Seeing myself without the buffer of the junk I was holding on to was jarring, but at least I had a tiny seed of hope. I got dressed, and she drove me to my appointment.

On the way to the hospital, Carmen's cell phone rang.

"Hold on. Here he is," she said, passing me her phone.

"Hey, Joe, how are you doing?" the voice on the other end said. It was Kim. She and her husband, Alfred, were our first friends in Atlanta. Ironically, Carmen and Kim met in 1985 when they worked at the Ridgeview Institute, the same hospital we were driving to.

"What time is your appointment?" she asked, as if she had a plan.

"Ten o'clock."

"Okay, we are going to start praying for you at 9:55."

"But, Kim," I interjected, "something happened last night." I went on to explain how I had felt as if I were being filled with a cool liquid and how it flowed up through my body and then overflowed out of me. Then she asked a question no one had ever asked me before. In fact, I had never even heard the phrase before.

"Was it like scales falling from your eyes?"

How can she know that? How can she nail it like that? And how can I even know what that meant?

"Yes, that's exactly what it was like!" I said with a big smile on my face.

The first order of business before you're admitted to a psychiatric hospital is the all-important evaluation, the part where they decide if you're crazy enough to join their club. A few days in, I asked one of the doctors if I really needed to be there. He gave me an odd look and said sternly, "You don't get into this place unless you really need it."

I remember a sweet girl taking me into a small room for the interview even though my wife and other doctors had already told them enough to create a file on me an inch thick. I guess they needed to hear crazy from the horse's mouth to make it official.

"So, tell me what's been going on," she said.

I launched into it and watched as she took notes, her head bent over the forms, occasionally nodding. When I finished, she did a quick recap.

"So, we have an episode of severe depression and anxiety combined with some abuse of medications and some past alcohol abuse… Is there anything else?"

She flipped the page and her hair in one fluid motion and waited for me to respond, her eyes looking down at the sheet to make sure everything was in order. She had done this a thousand times.

I was just about cleared for takeoff, and she had to ask, "Is there anything else?" Of course there was something else. *Only the biggest thing that has ever happened to me!* But then, it was all new to me. I didn't know how to describe it, and I was afraid I might project the wrong kind of crazy, the kind that lands you in a straitjacket. Tears suddenly flooded my eyes.

"I think I was visited by God last night," I said softly. Her pen paused in midair. She looked up at me as if instead of "God" I had said "Elvis."

"Really?" she said in her best nonjudgmental voice. "Why don't you tell me about that?"

I gave her a detailed account. The more I talked about it, the more I began to understand the weight of what had happened. I cried a little more. When I was done, she handed me a tissue and checked me in.

I attended the outpatient program Monday through Friday, spending the majority of the time in a classroom setting. Large-group discussions covered everything from the causes of depression to pharmacology, coping skills, and physical fitness. In smaller groups we talked about our individual issues. The first day I met my main counselor. He didn't seem like a good fit at first, mostly because he had a habit of wearing his crew-neck sweater with his shirt collar on the outside. It bugged me. I became preoccupied with it. Maybe part of me was resisting all this. As long as I stayed hung up on some stupid detail like a shirt collar, I wouldn't have to work on getting better.

He turned out to be the perfect counselor.

The first time we met privately, he shared a big chunk of his story, and I could relate to much of what he said. He started slipping me little pieces of paper with strange lettering: "Rom 12:1, Phi 4:8, Rom 8:28." He was a former professional football player, so I thought this was the snap count. "Rome 121, Phi 48, Rome 828—hut, hut!" After he saw the confusion in my eyes, he explained it to me.

I went home and looked up the verses in my mom's old King James. In the book of Romans, chapter 12, verse 1: "Present your bodies a living sacrifice, holy, acceptable unto God."

In the book of Philippians, chapter 4, verse 8: "Finally, brethren, whatsoever things are true, whatsoever things are honest, whatsoever things are just, whatsoever things are pure, whatsoever things are lovely, whatsoever things are of good report; if there be any virtue, and if there be any praise, think on these things."

Also in the book of Romans, chapter 8, verse 28: "And we know that all things work together for good to them that love God, to them who are the called according to his purpose."

It somehow made sense to me.

At my first group meeting, I sat in one of the chairs that lined the walls of the windowless room and watched as the other patients shuffled in. They seemed like a fairly normal bunch. One by one they all said their names and described how they were feeling that day. The counselors gave out a list of alternate words to use to describe our feelings. I guess "good" and "fine" and "okay" were too pedestrian. Apparently, the approved list of words had a track record of cutting through the manure. (I was particularly fond of *sparkly* and *fuzzy*.)

When everyone else had finished, the counselor turned to me and said, "So, Joe, why don't you tell us why you're here?"

I heard words come out of my mouth that had never come out before.

"I think I'm here to serve you all." To say this was so out of character for me; it was akin to saying Hannibal Lecter was now a vegetarian. I don't think I had ever served anyone. I liked luxury hotels and expensive sheets with high thread counts and the service that came with five stars and many diamonds. I wasn't someone who thought about other people's needs. I expected to be served. This was one more layer of skin I would shed in the coming months.

A few weeks into my treatment, family members were invited in as part of the program. Even children. Our girls were ten and thirteen at the time, and we decided that we didn't want to expose them completely to what was going on. It was important to both of us to preserve their childhood innocence for as long as possible. We sat down with them and explained that Daddy wasn't feeling well and was going to spend some time getting healthy. I thought it would leave a mark on our ten-year-old and could be crushing to her.

"Girls, do you have any questions for Daddy or me?" Carmen asked after we were finished. I took a deep breath and waited for questions that might be difficult to answer. *Is Daddy crazy? Is he going to leave us?* The kind of questions that break your heart because they are so honest.

My little one's big brown eyes were as wide as I had ever seen them as she took it all in. She was such a delicate flower. Truly the sweetest person I have ever known. Now her pretty face was serious. Imagining the questions she would ask and the deep wounds they might reveal, I fought to hold back my tears.

"What are we having for dinner?" she asked.

14. THE GOOD NEWS

I had never felt so alive. The sun was brighter. Food tasted better. I was able to follow through with things. I listened instead of thinking about what I was going to say next. I felt no need to prepare a defense of myself. I really heard what people were saying, and as a result I felt connected. I was present with the people in my life.

I know—cue the Pepsi commercial. But it was true, and if anyone had wanted me to do a commercial for this new life of mine, I would have. Something had happened to me, and I noticed it from the inside out. It started that night when the darkness I had known for so long was replaced with light. My addictions vanished in an instant. No compulsions, no cravings.

It was—please, no snickering—a miracle. My compass had been recalibrated. I immediately quit swearing. I wasn't consciously trying not to swear; it just didn't come out of me any longer. I even started to obey traffic laws. I couldn't speed anymore! Before, I had gone 120 miles per hour every time I drove to the office. Now, if the sign said no right turn on red, then I couldn't turn right on red!

What was going on? I didn't know. But I also didn't care. It was good.

From the outside, my life looked like a shipwreck. I was on leave from my job. My days were spent at a psychiatric hospital. My wife had watched me go off the deep end and didn't know what to think. This was the opposite of how things were just months before when the outside looked so perfect and my insides were filled with maggots. Now, from the outside it seemed I was a mess, while on the inside I was filled with the peace of God.

I was drawn to finding out as much as I could about God and spiritual things. I picked up a book that had been collecting dust on my nightstand: *The Purpose Driven Life* by Rick Warren. It became a textbook to me. I finished it in two days instead of the recommended forty. I reread it several times over the course of the next few months. I bought the audio version and listened to it over and over. I started giving away copies to anyone who would accept them from me.

Naturally, my daughters concluded that aliens had taken up residence in my body. They were used to the cool guy who let them watch MTV, *Saturday Night Live,* and most everything else on TV and online. It freaked them out that I was now policing their TV and music for anything unhealthy or offensive. If to them I was now more present and stable than Old Dad had been, in other ways they didn't like New Dad quite so much.

I stayed in the outpatient program for five weeks with my boss's blessing. But I soon decided that the five-week hiatus from work wasn't enough. I needed a longer break. I decided to leave the job that had been waiting for me.

"What are you going to do?" someone from my group asked me before I left. "You know, for money?"

"I don't have any idea," I said. "But I'm sure God will take care of us."

"Wow! You really are in a good place, aren't you?" he said.

"Yes, I am." I meant it.

I had only one goal that summer: to *not* work. Of course, all kinds of people call when you don't want a job, and I was contacted by several entrepreneurs to see if I would join them. One such media gent pitched me a cowboy channel: "All Cowboy, All the Time." Another had an idea for an emergency-alert system via cell phone. One showed me a speakerphone device shaped like a hockey puck.

I had never before been good about rejecting ideas and opportunities, but now I was determined to give myself some time to find out how my life had become such a mess. I didn't want to jump back into the rat race again. I wanted to hang on to this peace and stability I'd found. So I said no to everything (even though I actually kind of liked the cowboy-channel idea).

One of the requirements for discharge from the hospital program was a written plan. You had to show them you could stay healthy on the outside before they turned you loose. You also had to arrange to continue therapy with an outside counselor. I would have gladly stayed a few more weeks. I wanted to know as much as I could about how a person can get so far off track, and they were handing out the answers like candy on Halloween. But my insurance ran out, so I had to go whether I was ready or not.

Even though it had been an outpatient program, getting officially discharged felt like a return home. It was a step back onto the terra firma of Real Life, which was both exciting and a bit unsettling to me.

After I left the program, I began to see a therapist twice a week. She asked me to write down everything I could remember about growing up. She wanted me to explore every dusty, cobwebbed, boarded-up corner of my heart and mind. When we looked at what filled the pages, the memories were almost exclusively unhappy ones. I had a hard time recalling many happy childhood memories, which made me angry. The therapist taught me to be patient, to let those feelings wash over me instead of trying to make them go away. Of course, the latter had always been my customary method for handling pain.

Some weeks before, Joshua had given me a Bible.

We had other Bibles in our house, but frankly they had been just books for the bookshelf, nothing I would open up and actually read.

This was different. When Joshua handed it to me, I took it like a drowning man reaching for a life preserver. This was the first Bible that I cared about. It called my name. It was God saying to me, "Joe, here I am."

Joshua had taken me under his wing. I am astonished now by how much time he spent with me, first while I was in the hospital, then later during those first weeks and months of my new life. He arranged his schedule so he could get together with me a few nights a week.

We'd read Scripture together, I'd try to make sense of it, and then Joshua would explain what things meant. I had no idea what he was talking about most of the time. He would jump from one book to another. I didn't understand why we didn't just read it front to back.

As clueless as I was, Joshua was infinitely patient, and his quiet passion walked me into the presence of God in His Word. No one will ever convince me angels don't exist. Joshua was one. I felt so good hanging out with him, talking about God, and experiencing the amazing truths in a Bible that I felt was written to me.

15. THE TV NEWS

The story—or parts of the story—of the fishermen hit the newswires August 16, 2006, and traveled around the world in an instant.

One of the world's oldest news agencies, Reuters, was among the first organizations to report the rescue. They speculated that the three fishermen could have been lost for almost a year. They also referenced earlier reports suggesting the fishermen had been lost for about three months. Reuters explained that some facts remained sketchy due to language difficulties between the Mexican men and the Taiwanese crew who'd rescued them. *China Daily* and the *Taiwan Journal* ran the feed and added the familiar comparisons, calling it a twenty-first-century *Robinson Crusoe* story.

Once the story was on the newswires, it was picked up in quick succession by the BBC, ABC, NBC, CBS, FOX, and scores of other outlets, including ESPN. MSNBC quoted Jesús as saying, "We never lost hope because there is a God up there."[2] The story made its way to the evangelical Christian magazine *Christianity Today,* where Jesús was quoted as saying, "We spent most of the time reading the Bible…fishing and praying mostly. God really helped us because we were at sea for so long."[3]

The Mexican Council of Bishops said the fishermen's faith was a shining example to others.

All the major news agencies of Mexico immediately flew to the South Pacific. Each wanted to be first to speak to the men. Many reporters rented small boats and went out to sea in search of the rescue ship while it was still making its way to port. They found it about an hour out. The men were standing on the deck of the *Koos 102,* emaciated and sunburned with skin peeling off their faces.

After what seemed like an eternity, the Taiwanese trawler pulled into the port city of Majuro. Majuro is part of the Marshall Islands, east of the Philippines, north of New Zealand, and southwest of Hawaii. In short, it's not close to anything but is in the middle of the vast Pacific.

In borrowed clothing, the men stood on the deck of the trawler as it eased into port. His trusty Casio watch still on his wrist, Lucio wore a long-sleeve black shirt, black baseball cap, and sweatpants. Jesús stood tall in black sweats and a purple short-sleeve Reebok sports jersey with the Sacramento Kings logo on the front. Salvador looked as though he could go to work on casual Friday, wearing a beige short-sleeve Tommy Bahama–style shirt and black pants.

Despite their borrowed clothes, the men bore the marks of life-and-death survival. They were so weak they had to swing their arms back and up, for momentum, in order to shield their sun-dried eyes when looking into the distance. They appeared solemn as the reality of their survival seemed to be sinking in. Soon they heard a familiar accent coming from the reporters shouting questions, and smiles crept onto each face.

While still on board the boat, the fishermen were greeted with a handshake from a woman who acted as a kind of grand marshal. She presented each man with a headdress of flowers in the colors of the Mexican flag as a gesture of congratulations and welcome. There was celebration in the port, as news of the fishermen's ordeal and rescue had preceded them; much like soldiers returning from battle, they had survived.

Finally the fishermen limped off the trawler. Their feet were so swollen they couldn't wear shoes. Barefoot, they headed gingerly down the plank to dry land, setting foot on firm ground for the first time in ten months.

Immediately the media—with TV cameras, tripods, booms, handheld microphones, and recording devices—started running toward them. One reporter had gotten a picture of Jesús's new baby girl, born while he was at sea. The photo was passed along by other reporters until it was shown to Jesús. He was overcome with tears. The reporter who supplied the picture glanced back to make sure his cameraman was capturing the moment.

Someone handed a cell phone to Lucio, and within seconds he was talking with his family. He spoke with Panchita, his eighty-year-old grandmother, whose faith had been unwavering. When she heard his voice on the other end, she knew: her constant prayers had been answered.

The men were helped up into the back of an ambulance, which drove off toward a medical center where they would be checked out.

The authorities in Majuro and those from the Mexican embassy in New Zealand busily worked out details for the fishermen's return to Mexico; even so, that would take some time. So the fishermen would have to remain in Majuro for a few days. Meanwhile, they got their land legs back. They were treated kindly by the locals and were genuinely humbled by the people's generosity. They were given clothing and offered meals. The hotel and restaurant employees were honored to be able to serve them.

It was still strange for them to consume anything other than fish and blood. But they soon began to enjoy the fruits of civilization. One of the fishermen's first sit-down dinners on land consisted of cheeseburgers, Cokes, and chocolate cake with vanilla ice cream for dessert. This was, in fact, the meal they had fantasized about while at sea. Better than the smell of pancakes and cigarettes. It was like experiencing a new sense as their taste buds reactivated after nearly a year of turtle blood and the gristly chew of raw meat.

It would be the beginning of a new kind of hunger for each of the men, one that few can truly understand—much like being a prisoner of war. The atrophy of the body without proper nutrition, exercise, and medical attention is a common occurrence for POWs. The eyes start to fail, and diseases and maladies—scurvy, beriberi, diarrhea—set in.

During their odyssey their appetites shrank to a point that it took very little to satisfy the hunger pangs. But back on land with so many choices and such large quantities of food available, the men ate as if they would never get to eat again. Understandable for them, but for others of us looking to fill the emptiness inside, that behavior catches up to us quickly.

The men were not asked where in Mexico their return destinations should be, so as the authorities made travel arrangements, it was assumed that each should be sent to what was deemed to be his hometown.

Salvador's birthplace was Oaxaca. Oaxaca is a state in south-central Mexico near Guatemala. It's named after the *guaje* tree. During the 1970s and '80s the guaje was promoted as a "miracle tree" for its multiple uses as hardwood for floors, carvings for necklaces, and a vegetable for human consumption. Oaxaca was also a hotbed of political activity; just before the men were rescued, it was the location of an uprising over the presidential elections. (Later the fishermen's rescue would figure into the intrigue surrounding the highly controversial political race.)

But Salvador hadn't lived in Oaxaca for a long time. While it was his birth city, it was also some sixteen hours southeast from where he'd spent most of his childhood years. It had been ages since he'd seen any of his family who lived there. No one there would know him.

How different it would be for Lucio, whose hometown was the tiny village El Limon, close to San Blas, where a massive celebration was already being planned. In fact, all the neighboring villages and towns were being notified that Lucio Rendon of nearby El Limon was one of the returning heroes known as the *tres pescadores,* and an area-wide party was going to take place in San Blas as soon as they could get him back home.

A similarly large event was being planned for Jesús's arrival at the Culiacán airport, ninety minutes northeast of his little village of Las Arenitas. He had left behind his parents, siblings, young pregnant wife, and three-year-old son. They had agonized over his disappearance, finally coming to the conclusion that he was gone forever. They had buried him and said their good-byes.

Now he was miraculously returning.

Of course, in Majuro the fishermen had no knowledge of what was being planned. They restlessly awaited their return flights home. Reporters seemed insatiable. Cameras watched each move the fishermen made, hovering around them at all possible moments. The fishermen didn't mind; they were just happy to be anywhere but on the Pacific. They made many new Spanish-speaking friends, mostly from the media.

Earlier on the Taiwanese trawler, they hadn't spoken with anyone. None of the crew spoke Spanish. The fishermen never told anyone on board that they started from Mexico with a crew of five. Now when it was mentioned in the company of their new Spanish-speaking friends, jaws dropped. The fishermen didn't notice.

They allowed authorities to take care of all the logistics. None of the fishermen had ever traveled outside of Mexico, and now they were halfway around the world, trying to get home. Once all the bookings were done, they packed up the few possessions given to them on the rescue ship and in Majuro.

Just two personal items survived their ordeal on the Pacific. Lucio strapped on his Casio watch. And Salvador carefully picked up his Bible, wrapped it in a towel, and slipped it into a Ziploc bag.

16. Peace and Pain

As Joshua and I sat one evening in the same restaurant where he had prayed for me, I hunched down low across the table. "Does everybody who knows God have this feeling?" I whispered. "And if they do, why aren't they telling other people about it? Because, I'm just sayin', this is unbelievable!"

The "feeling," as I called it, was so clear and clean. I had never experienced anything like it. No high I had ever been on was even close. It was uncontaminated, almost sparkling, and I sensed I was connected in some way to something otherworldly or supernatural. I required less sleep and would spring out of bed early in the morning long before sunrise, hoping that more would be revealed each day. I had no worries about next year, next month, or even next week. I was living moment by moment, and I loved it.

"You're lucky," Joshua said, laughing. "Stretch out in it. Most people never feel this."

And I did. Certainly it helped that I was jobless. No rat race to slide back into. Better than a vacation (which I always spent thinking about work anyway), this period of time was a total stop for me, and it gave me an opportunity to breathe, laugh, and see life in a whole new way.

And so that summer I stretched. I felt joy in a way I never had before. I know how strange that sounds to others. Before this, I could not have fathomed the concept of joy and would hardly have known what it truly was. Before, when I'd heard others say what I was now saying, I would be dismissive and think of it as gooey spiritual talk. But *this*—this was real. It was like the rush you get after a hard workout or a brisk morning run, yet this wasn't about endorphins, much less artificially manufactured substances. This was about a real, true spiritual release, the chemistry of God's grace that substituted His "enoughness" for my relentless needs and drives.

One of the big questions of course was, what would Carmen do with me?

At first, my new relationship with God looked to her like everything else I'd gone through. She had every right to be skeptical. I'm sure she was afraid that this spiritual transformation was just another one of my passing fancies, like juicing, or the South Beach Diet, or the marathon I decided to run even though I had never run any kind of race before. She must have recalled the time I ordered a hundred boxes of green tea online because I thought it wasn't available in stores. So I had a history, and "spiritual transformation" must have seemed to her like another in a series of delusional events. After all, she had never observed a conversion like this. The only exposure either of us had in this area was to a TV preacher knocking some poor guy in the head and yelling, "You're healed!"

But though she had reasonable doubt, she stuck with me, perhaps hopeful that this latest pursuit of mine was something different, more, and real. She gave me space, and I will be forever grateful for that.

Being able to see my life through fresh eyes was what brought me guilt and grief. I now could see clearly how much I had missed.

I was only beginning to understand the enormous sacrifices Carmen had made throughout our marriage. She had done it all herself, and I don't mean making beds and tying hair ribbons. She had been carrying our family on her back for years, making excuses to friends for my erratic behavior, polishing up the surface of our lives that the world saw, holding in the pain I had caused. It broke my heart to think that she had, in effect, been alone for fifteen years. I realize now that Carmen and I are not terminally unique in this way; many marriages are the same.

It was time for me to become the husband she deserved and the man God had created me to be. I knew I could profess complete transformation and talk about miracles all day long, but the only way I was going to convince Carmen that I had changed was to show her a new man. I didn't pray for God to change *her;* instead, I prayed for God to change *me.* We went back to a counselor we had seen before and started working on *us.*

What was shocking to me was that for all those years I hadn't seen anything or anyone around me. I had been focused straight ahead. I thought I could continue chasing success until—well, until I didn't know when. But I sure wasn't going to slow down to figure it out. The self-deception was that I could make it all work. I think most men have this blind spot.

We create our own truth.

My truth had been me. As long as I could deliver the goods, it would all be okay. But then it quit working. My truth quit working. Suddenly I couldn't deliver the goods, and there wasn't much use for me.

With my whole life and identity tied up in my work and whom I knew and what I possessed, there was no solid foundation to stand on. I had built my life on a cornerstone of flesh—me—and heaped everything I had acquired on top of it. Eventually I couldn't stand the weight of it all, and my life crumbled like a house of sand. And then everything I had fell into a pile of useless stuff.

It saddened me that I had been absent in one way or another for so many important moments in my girls' lives. I had bought into the "kids are resilient" lie; I thought that I could hide my behaviors and make up time away with gifts from each trip. I used the old "quality time" rationalization. When it came to my drinking, I used the old "do as I say, not as I do" routine. Now I knew better. Nothing makes up for not being there.

The impact of my choices was revealed when my older daughter wrote me a letter to tell me how much it meant to her that I had gotten sober. She had been away at a middle-school church retreat, and all the kids were asked to write about something special or significant in their lives. While other kids wrote about their pets or getting their first cell phone, my daughter wrote a heart-wrenching essay on the agony and sorrow that was me, how I had been oblivious to what my drinking had inflicted upon her young life. She described how terrified she was when I got drunk, then how happy she was when I quit drinking. She called it the most important thing that had happened in her life.

This was for me painfully bittersweet. I felt joy that, because I was sober now, she was embracing me for it. I also felt regret, knowing my little girl had an earlier picture of me on the mantel of her mind. Nothing counts for much when you've hurt your own daughter—and never even knew it.

17. THE SUMMER OF JOE

I t was the "summer of Joe."

I finished reading the Bible for the first time. The whole thing. My new craving was for a greater knowledge and understanding of this new life, and I read nothing but the Word of God. I read it every day. I started on page 1 and read all the way to the back cover, just as though I was reading a regular book. Then I got a different translation and read that one. Then another. Somehow, it was feeding me.

During the course of my reading, I came across a passage that jumped out at me. It was in the book of Ezekiel. The phrase "stand in the gap" hit my eyes, my mind, and my heart in a split second, and it spoke to me. It prompted me to write it down and vow to somehow stand in the gap too. I wasn't sure what it meant, so I tucked it away in the nightstand and didn't give it much more thought.

I joined a neighborhood men's Bible study. I realized they had been inviting me by e-mail every other week for a couple of years. Now, instead of deleting the e-mail, I answered it.

At the meetings I started to reveal myself in a way I had never done before. It felt awkward at first but was incredibly freeing. My personal story dribbled out in bits and pieces until one day the study leader prompted me point-blank: "So tell us what happened."

I got all tight and twitchy at first, then just let loose. Guys don't usually talk this way to other guys. Our invisible force field detects any incoming and outgoing emotions and zaps them instantly. This seemed like a different crowd, though. They welcomed me openly in spite of what I'd done and gone through.

I learned that everyone has a story.

One of the guys from the study invited Carmen and me to an event with him and his wife. It was on a Saturday night at a new church located in an old grocery store. That sounded strange, but we liked the couple, so we went anyway. That night we found ourselves in the middle of a variety show. There was a band that played eighties music, a troupe that did sketch comedy, and an abundance of brownies. We sat at one of the fifty large round tables and listened and laughed. I had never experienced anything like that at a church before, and I decided to go back the next day for the Sunday service.

In the daylight I noticed a simple sign on the building: Buckhead Church. I walked in, a few people greeted me, and I slid into one of the rows—not pews—in the same room that the night before had been like a room at Caesars Palace. But now it was set up like a giant theater, and just as dark. The service began with another incredible band playing louder than the one the night before. It felt like a concert, and I think I even saw some smoke and strobe lights. When the music ended, I fully expected to see people waving cigarette lighters over their heads. Instead, an usher passed an offering plate and told first-timers not to give anything. I thought, *Wow. This is my kind of church—rock music and no pressure to give money.* Then an enormous movie screen dropped down at center stage, and a video sermon began (the pastor was streamed from another location). His message was awesome. I was sitting in a rock-and-roll, grocery-store, video church—and I liked it.

If "the summer of Joe" meant to God that He was finally getting my attention, it meant to Carmen and the girls that they had me, completely and fully present, for perhaps the first time ever.

We spent many of the weekends that summer at a lake ninety minutes from our house. Carmen's parents had found a bargain and bought a cottage as an investment. We loved it so much we bought our own lake house a hundred yards away. We did watersports; the girls learned to wakeboard; we played golf and tennis together; we read books. We lived.

And of all the good activities I enjoyed with Carmen and the kids during the summer of Joe, there was something I loved most of all: I would pray, go out on the lake by myself, and listen for God.

The cottage became our refuge, a place where it was just us, together. The time we spent there, especially because we were in close quarters with each other on the boat or in the cottage, was for me heaven on earth. I never assumed I could make up for lost time, but this was time now, with them.

I had finally come home.

18. *Dichos de Mi Madre*

A good friend called to say there were some people he thought I should meet.

A group was developing family-friendly content in the publishing industry, and they were looking for someone with my media experience. Though I didn't know much about publishing, the idea of creating books intrigued me. So we sat down and talked.

After several meetings I found myself accepting a position in charge of distribution.

There were many ways this didn't make sense. It was a noble-enough venture but not really my thing. "Media distribution" sounded as if it mapped into my previous experience pretty well, but in fact it was a completely different world. My thing had been TV syndication; this was publishing. Also, this was a start-up operation, and while I liked some aspects of "small," I was used to the size, clout, and resources of big media corporations. Further, I didn't know anything about children's resources and educational materials.

Frankly, I wasn't sure why I had said yes to the job. But I had. And now I know why.

It was there that I would meet someone who would unexpectedly change my life—again.

❧

An old friend I knew from my TV days called to say there was someone we should talk to, a woman with a children's book project.

Her name was Victoria. She was older (though I could never tell how old) with silver hair, stood five feet tall, and weighed less than a hundred pounds. She was Jewish and had been raised in Bogotá, Colombia. Her late husband had been a high-ranking executive at Coca-Cola, and before he died a year earlier, he had written a book that Victoria wanted us to publish.

I liked Victoria's spunk; I also found myself drawn to something else about her. When each meeting was finished, everyone but Victoria and me would leave the room. We would sit and talk, and I loved her beautiful reverence when she spoke about God.

We felt that the original book proposal she pitched to us wasn't a good fit, but we liked a second idea she mentioned: *Dichos de Mi Madre.* "The Sayings of My Mother." It was to be a little gift book with about three hundred Spanish sayings, targeted to Latinos. Victoria saw the book as a gift that could be passed from one generation to the next; it was her small effort to keep some of her culture alive. We saw it as something that could give us an easy entry into that market, something we could also expand to other languages. I threw my yes on the pile, and we agreed to move forward toward publication.

I now know that things don't "just happen," but when we're in the middle of them, we don't always know what's really going on or why.

It happened during one of the subsequent meetings with Victoria. The business discussion had ended, and the rest of the team had left the conference room. She and I were talking about God and His people. As usual, I was fascinated not only by the content of our conversation but also by her deep spirituality.

We each had to go and attend to other things, so we said our good-byes until the next meeting. But as Victoria walked out the door of the conference room, she paused, turned back, and said, "Joe, have you heard about the Mexican fishermen?"

It didn't ring a bell.

"Three Mexican fishermen were just rescued near Australia after drifting six thousand miles for almost ten months on a tiny boat. It's an amazing story."

I think my mind had already moved on to other business I had to get done. I just looked at her blankly. I wasn't getting it.

She continued, "They said they survived on raw fish, rainwater...and their *faith in God.*"

I started to tune in.

"And, Joe, on the boat the thing that survived the storm was a book—a Bible. Story is, they read it over and over."

She had my full attention now.

"I saw it on Univision last night," she said. "Look it up on the computer, if you like."

I slid over to one of the computers and Googled it while Victoria watched from the doorway. I found a link and saw the story: three men rescued at sea. I saw the quote about raw fish and faith.

"Isn't it an amazing story, Joe?" Victoria asked.

I nodded, although I wasn't really responding to her. Something about the story was already resonating within me. I knew I would come back to it later and read more about guys who were lost, sustained by the words of a Bible, then rescued after a long time adrift.

But for now I had other things to do. I got up and started toward my office, but Victoria wouldn't let me go. She zeroed in. "Do you think you could get it, Joe? Could you get the story?"

Whatever my interest in the fishermen's ordeal might be personally, I didn't see myself going after the story as a business proposition.

"Victoria," I said, "everyone will be after this story."

She was undaunted.

"It would be a great story to have, Joe." She paused and then said, "My nephew could help you. He lives in Mexico City. He's a lot like you, Joe, a real go-getter. He's very religious. Can I give my nephew your information?"

Frankly, I had already moved on. "Sure," I said, playing along.

With that, Victoria left the office. I was pretty sure I wouldn't hear another word about the fishermen ever again.

19. Undertow

C arnem and I had planned to go to the lake that weekend.
Summer was nearly over, and we wanted one last family hurrah
before the madness of the girls' school year set in. We wanted
to leave Friday around noon, so I crammed a day's worth of work into the
morning and was able to wrap things up by eleven thirty.

Just before I left, Victoria called. Her nephew Eli (pronounced EL-ee)
was planning to drive from Mexico City to San Blas, the port from which the
fishermen had departed in October of 2005. It was an eleven-hour drive, but
Victoria said he would be in touch when he got there.

Be in touch? I really didn't see what my role was. Had I indicated to her
that I was all that interested?

Carmen drove so I could get some work done on my computer. While in
the car, I got an e-mail from Eli. He was trying to make sense of the fishermen's story and wanted to know what to say if he found any of the survivors
or any family members in San Blas.

As a favor to Victoria, I e-mailed Eli some of my thoughts on the story. My first impression was that the story was truly miraculous, if indeed it was true. I wrote that if this was a story about faith, he should pursue that angle. "If it would inspire people," I said, "that would be good." The world needed it.

Once we arrived at the lake, I forgot about the fishermen for the rest of the day.

We had invited some friends to join us. Their eight-year-old boy went by the nickname of Smackers. We got the boat, threw Smackers and my girls into a giant pizza-slice-shaped tubing device, and did our very best to get them airborne. After a few hours of pounding their bodies with waves, we headed back to shore, got cleaned up, threw some burgers on the grill, and chilled.

Later we played monster golf with colossal plastic golf clubs and a golf ball the size of a small pumpkin. Then we settled in and played board games like Sorry!, Candy Land, Operation, and Twister.

This was my new life, and I loved it.

The next morning we got out on the boat again and headed across the water to a lakeside tennis club with a pool, water slide, and fitness room. Carmen and I went to the gym while the kids swam.

While I was working out, my mind drifted back to the fishermen. There was something intriguing about the story, but I couldn't put my finger on it. I had no business getting involved. The story didn't really fit the publishing house. Yet I had a strange sense that it fit *me* somehow. At the very least, I needed to read more about it.

After my workout I asked the receptionist if I could use the computer. Again I Googled the story about the fishermen. The entire first page of search results was now filled with headlines from all over the world. The story had taken off.

Before dinner that night, I logged on to my laptop. Now there were three pages of articles. It had quickly become global news.

On the way home the next day, I got another e-mail from Eli. His father had told him it was too dangerous to drive across Mexico alone. He wouldn't be making the trip to San Blas after all.

Just as I hadn't known why I'd taken the publishing job, this latest development tugged me in a way I couldn't explain. It was a pull, like the ocean's undertow. Something was happening inside me as I learned more about the fishermen and the remarkable story now exploding in the media. I knew this made no sense for me, but even though I tried to push it away, it kept consuming my thoughts.

This was different from times in the past when I had acted impulsively or compulsively, often irrationally. Now I was on solid ground, sober, stable, and more spiritually rooted than ever before. Somehow this thing that made no sense started to seem like precisely the right thing to do.

But that didn't mean it seemed right to anyone else in my life.

20. Plans

That night after we arrived home, Carmen approached me to confirm that I had the coming week's agenda for the girls on my calendar. This was going to be one of the six times a year she worked at the apparel mart. That meant seven straight twelve-hour days for her, and I was usually able to rearrange my schedule to help with carpooling and meals for the girls.

"So, you're able to help me out this week, right?" she asked. "I'm at the mart until Sunday."

She was not expecting my response. *I* was not expecting my response. It just came out of me. "You know what, honey. I don't think I'm going to be here for that."

She looked at me sideways.

"What? You aren't going to be here? We talked about this. Where are you going?"

"I think I have to go to Mexico." There was no denying it. The story that only days ago had seemed so foreign and far-fetched had taken up space in my heart. It was as if the decision had already been made and I simply walked into it. Perhaps that's how God's calls work, for me at least.

Carmen cocked her head to the other side, squared her jaw, and knit her eyebrows. Carmen doesn't explode; she fumes. She'll clench her teeth until the enamel grinds down a few layers. Then she'll let it out. It takes a lot to get her to that point, but I know it takes even more strength for her to keep her anger stuffed down. She had many years of practice, waking up each morning and wondering, *What will my husband do today?* Or, *What mess am I going to have to clean up now?*

I knew how this sounded. Another whacked-out Joe. Another mess. I hated that for even one second she would think that the change had worn off and that my new life had just been a fad. This wasn't at all fair to her, I knew.

I don't know how people make those choices. The choices that, in the moment, might seem unfair to those around them but must be made.

This was a tug, a pull, an undertow. Something bigger than I was, was at work here, and I just knew I had to do it. At that moment, as much as I loved Carmen and as much as I wanted her to trust the change in me, I had to follow the call.

"Remember the story of the Mexican fishermen I told you about?" I asked.

"What does that have to do with you?" she said, not smiling.

"I think I have to go to Mexico. I need to find them and meet them," I said. "I think there is something to this." She stood quietly for a few seconds, gazing at the wall a few inches to the left of my face. Then she fixed her eyes on me.

"Where exactly are you going?" she asked.

"I don't know."

"Who are you going to see?"

"I'm not sure."

"Joe, how are you going to talk to anyone? You don't even know the language!" Her voice was now an octave higher.

"I haven't figured that out yet," I said.

"Well, how long will you be gone?" she asked as her gaze returned to the same spot on the wall.

I paused, hating the truth of what I was about to say. "I don't know." At least I was honest. I waited. I wasn't going to change my mind, but I was willing to give her the last word.

It took her a while to utter it. But finally she looked at me, mustered what she could within her, and said, "If this is what you think you need to do, then…good luck."

To this day I don't know how she managed to say that. It took all she had.

21. FAITH

I had decided to fly to Mexico City, where Victoria's nephew lived. When I landed there, I called to check in at work. One of the partners told me they had discussed it further, and they weren't going to be part of this. I was on my own.

I had to let go of the idea that I had to understand it all, that it had to be rationalized in a way that could make sense to everyone, myself included. For once I was not obsessed with everything having to be sensible and completely understood down to the last detail. Having a complete understanding doesn't always take us to the place where we want or ought to go.

So I didn't try to rationalize to my colleagues why I had gone. At least not then. To myself I could say, *I'm in publishing, after all, so it makes sense to see if there is a book in this. . . . And all those years in the studio, well, I can't let that go to waste, right?* But I knew better. It looked as if I was going there to chase down the story. Perhaps land a contract for a book, maybe a movie. But really I *wasn't* going there for the story. I was following a call for an outcome I wouldn't control and couldn't imagine.

Eli picked me up in his Jeep Liberty and drove us to Polanco, a section of Mexico City similar to SoHo in New York.

Eli looked like a regular guy. He hadn't shaved in a while, he smoked cigarettes, and he drove like a New York cabby. We stopped for a bite and talked for about two hours. We connected right away, an orthodox Jew and a newbie Christian becoming friends over a kosher meal in Mexico. After lunch he gave me a lift back to the hotel so I could figure out what to do next. Flying to Mexico City was as far as my plan had gone.

I checked in at the front desk and scooped up three national newspapers from a table in the lobby. The coverage of the fishermen story was extensive, the story having grown since I'd last checked. Each paper had a front-page feature with many details inside. It seemed as if there was no other news— just the fishermen.

Back in my room, I turned on the television to find nonstop coverage, in Spanish of course. I sat on the end of the bed, staring at the screen.

I heard the word *canibalismo. Cannibalism?* I put my head in my hands and groaned. Had I come all the way to Mexico to chase down a story about man-eating fishermen? I called Eli, who said some of the authorities thought the three survivors had killed their two shipmates for food. That was bad enough. Then he told me about the drug rumors. "Maybe these guys weren't just poor fishermen who ran into some bad luck on the water," he said. "They may have been on a drug run." *What?* I had to get off the phone. It was too much to take in.

Over the next hour I tried to collect my thoughts and plot my next move. Considering these new developments, I had only one realistic alternative: go home. *And I thought I could come down here like some big-time investigative journalist and snag the story of the century.* It was crazy.

I searched online again. I noticed the town of San Blas repeated in several articles. It was where the fishermen's journey began. I Googled "San Blas." Believe it or not, this little village had a website. There was an ad for a hotel on it. The Garza Canela. I sent an e-mail asking if they had any rooms available, then went to sleep with drug-dealing cannibals on my mind.

Restless and awake at four the next morning, I turned on my computer and much to my surprise saw a message, in English, from Josefina, at the Garza Canela, confirming a room for one night and one night only. They were sold out through the weekend. I figured the press and the movie deal-makers had booked all the rooms. To have any hope of finding these men, I was going to need Josefina's help. I wrote back to her and emphasized that I wasn't some Hollywood producer out to serve my studio. I really believed that this story would be inspiring and maybe give hope to the village of San Blas and beyond. Maybe all of Mexico. Maybe the entire world. There was no question that this was a story about survival, but it was deeper than that. This was a story about faith and hope and more. Faith in the unseen. Hope that comes from character. Character that comes from perseverance. Perseverance that comes from suffering. Suffering that we all face.

Then I waited. I kept checking my e-mail and the connection to the wall. I paced the floor. By eight o'clock, I couldn't wait any longer. I called the Garza Canela, and Josefina answered. I identified myself and asked her why she hadn't responded to my message. "I am not at the front desk right now," she said. I found out later that Josefina was the hotel manager and that San Blas was in an earlier time zone than Mexico City. I recapped my e-mail message, and when I got to the part about hope, she cut me off.

"Oh. You need to come here," she said.

"Why do you say it like that?" I asked. She seemed to be implying something more.

"There is no hope in San Blas. There hasn't been any hope here for a long time, ever since my parents have owned this hotel. This story is the only thing giving hope to anyone."

No hope? Well, I have hope. I'll bring some of it right on down... "How do I get there?" I asked.

"I think the road is paved coming from Puerto Vallarta," she said.

Strangely, this was not comforting. "Where should I go as I leave the airport?" I asked as I grabbed a piece of paper and a pen and got ready for her directions.

"You get on the road right in front of the airport and go a few hours north," she said. "When you come to a flashing yellow light, turn left and go about another hour, hour and a half, toward the coast."

"Then what?"

"That's it."

That's it? Look for a yellow flashing light, and turn left?

"Maybe you could send me a map?" I asked.

"We don't have any maps!" She was starting to sound annoyed, so I asked her to go over the directions one more time in case I had missed anything. I hadn't. When I told her I would try to make it there by dark, she laughed.

"You must get here during the day," she said. "If you come after dark, you won't find anyone." Then she got serious. "Besides, it's very dangerous to drive through the jungle at night."

My hope was that somehow my path would be lit. I hung up the phone, got my stuff together, and thirty minutes later was standing at the front desk staring at a bill for forty-eight hundred pesos, about four hundred dollars.

Then it hit me. When I'd booked the room, I'd assumed I was spending company money. In fact most of my life I had spent company money. Now I was on my own. My quest was on my own dime. This was real money, coming from my own pocket. And this was just the beginning. There was going to be the airfare, a rental to drive to San Blas, my room there, plus the last-minute plane ticket I had bought to Mexico City, then rights fees, lawyers, agents, and who knew what else. I couldn't imagine what Carmen and the girls thought of me. And what about my publishing partners, who probably saw this as one of the worst wild-goose chases of all time? *What am I doing?*

I paid the bill, and by the time I had made my way through the lobby doors, I had changed my mind. I threw my bag of hope and Josefina under the bus and decided to go home and beg my wife for mercy, apologize to everyone, and forget all about the fishermen.

I got into the cab, and the doorman shut out the noise of Polanco. I stretched my legs and was about to begin crafting my apology when I heard on the radio, in English, "'Cause I gotta have faith…" The familiar notes of George Michael's song "Faith" filled the cab. *Come on! You must be kidding me.*

I called Eli and told him everything that happened after I heard about the cannibalism—about Josefina at the hotel, the hope, my doubts, the bill, my doubts, and the song.

"Am I crazy to think this is more than a coincidence?" I asked Eli. "Is God using George Michael to tell me something?"

"Joe, there are no coincidences," Eli said. "That's what this whole thing is about. Faith—the faith of the fishermen, your faith as a Christian, my faith as an orthodox Jew." He sounded confident, and I believed him.

I thought about it for a split second. "Okay, I'm back in," I said to Eli, to myself, and to God. "I'm going to San Blas."

The cabdriver took me to the international departure gate at the Mexico City airport, and it occurred to me that I must have looked like a complete gringo. He assumed I was leaving the country, and he probably thought that was a good idea. Fortunately, he spoke a little English and understood when I told him I needed to be taken to the domestic terminal instead.

"Which airline?" he asked. I had no idea.

"Which ones do you have? I need to go to Puerto Vallarta." He circled back around the airport to the domestic drop-off and helped me haul my gigantic bag out of the trunk. As he drove off, a kid approached me and motioned to my bag. Again, I'm sure it was because I looked like such a gringo.

"*No hablo español*," I said. "I need to get to Puerto Vallarta. *¿Habla inglés?*"

The kid shook his head but took my luggage inside where it seemed there were thousands of people. I scanned the crowd for a person who might possibly speak English, and when I didn't see anyone promising, I decided to check the flight monitors. An AeroMexico flight was leaving for Puerto Vallarta at noon. My watch said 10:50 a.m. There were later flights, but I was mindful of Josefina's cautions about driving through the jungle at night. I needed to get there ASAP. I looked around, hoping to find someone who might be able to help me, and spotted a man in a pilot's uniform.

"Excuse me," I said. "I'm trying to get to this little town called San Blas. Have you heard of it?"

He nodded.

"Is flying into Puerto Vallarta the best way to get there?"

"Mazatlán is much closer," he said with a heavy Mexican accent. "What are you going to be doing in San Blas?"

"Well," I said, "you've probably seen or read about the three fishermen who were rescued. I'm going there to try to find their families and—"

"What a hoax!" he said.

I was stunned. "What do you mean?"

"It's the government—they faked it. My father is a doctor, and he said there's no way anyone could survive that long at sea. It's impossible. He says their bodies would be destroyed. Did you see the pictures? They looked too healthy to have spent so many months on the water."

I'm sure by this point I had gone completely white, or maybe green.

"The government has created this story to take attention away from the elections," he said as if he knew it for a fact.

Imagine that, I thought. I picked my tongue up off the ground, muttered an anemic "thank you," and walked away. I was in a daze. He was so sure, and I was so unsure. My body felt as if it were split in two: one side saying, "Stick with it," the other side telling me to bag the whole thing. A guy in a uniform was telling me it was all lies. A voice on the other end of a phone line talked about hope. I ached with indecision. But for some reason, I kept moving toward the AeroMexico counter. Then I heard my disembodied voice say, "I need a ticket to Puerto Vallarta, the twelve o'clock flight, please."

The attendant looked at her screen. "There are no seats available for that flight, but I have something on the 2:30 p.m. flight that gets in to Puerto Vallarta at 4:00 p.m. Would you like me to book that for you?"

I began to calculate. *Four o'clock. That means I could be on the road by five at the earliest. It probably gets dark around six thirty or seven, but there's a one-hour time difference. The drive will take maybe four hours.* I thought about Josefina again.

"I really need to be on the twelve o'clock flight, but let me think about it for a minute." Again I thought this was it. Time to call it quits. Another roadblock, another indication that this was the end of the line. It didn't seem like the path was being lit very well. From where I stood, I could see the signs for the Delta terminal and the possibility of a flight straight home to Atlanta. It would be that easy.

I turned to walk away.

"Excuse me, sir," I heard the agent say. "A first-class seat just became available for the noon flight."

22. MACHINE GUNS AND A FLASHING YELLOW LIGHT

My seat on the plane, so miraculously provided, also had its downside. The first-class seat cost a lot of money. And now I was counting the price of everything in my head, realizing it was all on my own dime and worrying how I would finance it. I had already spent thousands of dollars. My job was perhaps in some jeopardy, my kids were in private school, and I owned two homes.

But then it happened. I felt a nudge, an impression, almost a voice, saying, *Joe, it's not your money. It's My money.* I immediately thought of a sermon series our pastor, Andy Stanley, had presented earlier that summer. My takeaway from it was that our money and everything else we have is God's. *Here I was, hearing and sensing the truth of that with crystal clarity.*

Immediately I felt a weight being lifted from me. Not that in days to come I wouldn't worry from time to time about expenses, but the nudge was God's affirmation that I was where He wanted me and that I needed to press on.

After landing in Puerto Vallarta, I found myself staring at a royal blue Ford Fiesta rental in the middle of a dusty parking lot.

"Do you have another map?" I asked the car-rental agent, pointing to the local map of Puerto Vallarta that Hertz had provided. "I need a map of the country."

"That's all we have," she said. "Where are you going?"

"San Blas, north of here."

"It's easy to find." She pointed to the road between the car lot and the airport. "You take this road and keep going for about three hours until you see a flashing yellow light. Turn left at the light and follow the signs."

Again with the flashing yellow light? "What if the light's not working?" I asked. It seemed like a reasonable question.

"Oh, it's working," she said cheerfully. "It's always working."

I squeezed into the Fiesta and tried to psych myself up for the drive, a three-to-five-hour expedition through the jungle in search of three men I didn't know. *Don't have a map. Don't speak the language. Don't know a soul. Great. Just great.*

I pulled out of the parking lot and onto Highway 200, thankful I could still drive a stick. A few minutes later I stopped at a convenience store to buy some Diet Coke. (I love Diet Coke, and somehow the Diet Coke in Mexico is way better than the Diet Coke in the US.) When I walked in, I was immediately aware of my foreignness. This was real Mexico, not the fake, touristy, English-speaking Mexico, and it made me uneasy. A little farther down the road, I came to a security checkpoint where men with machine guns were stopping every car. *What have I gotten myself into?* I inched forward until one of the armed soldiers circled the Fiesta and then tapped on my window. I rolled it down gingerly, trying to look innocent while expecting to be shot to death at any moment.

"No hablo español," I said to the soldier. I repeated the phrase in English, hoping he would understand my midwestern accent better than my eighth-grade Spanish. Maybe he understood, or maybe I just looked too frightened to be a criminal, but after peering around the interior of the car, he waved me on.

About forty-five minutes into the drive, I started looking for the flashing yellow light. Both Josefina and the Hertz lady had said it would take me several hours to reach that landmark, but I wanted to make sure I didn't miss it. I didn't want to end up in south Texas. *Flashing yellow light. Flashing yellow light.* It became my inner mantra.

The twisting road through the jungle was quiet except for the grinding of gears when I shifted up or down. I flipped on the radio and heard an explosion of horns, accordions, and guitars, of the traditional Mexican banda. It was a psychotic, cartoonish soundtrack of all my fears that nearly gave me a heart attack. I batted at the radio knob to shut it off.

The noise was still ringing in my ears when I saw the machetes.

Sometimes talking to God can be exhausting. You pour your heart out, beg Him for something, anything, and it's almost as if He's up there in His La-Z-Boy reading the paper, nodding. And if He ever looks up, to prove He's really listening and not just reading the comics, you can't see it. It's like having a pen pal who never writes back.

Anyway, there I was, staring at ten rough-looking guys who were walking together and swinging two-foot-long blades, cutting brush that had grown up alongside the road. Had my path just gone completely dark?

"What am I doing here?" I asked God, which seemed to be a perfectly normal question. "Why would You send me on a wild-goose chase for these men if they're cannibals or drug dealers?" I was shouting now. "If this is not what You want me to be doing, then please show me! Run me off the road. Flatten a tire. Topple a tree in front of this car. Because, God, if You don't stop me, I'm just going to keep on with this."

No sooner had I uttered the words than butterflies began to circle the car. I don't mean just a few. It was a swarm, and then a swarm of swarms — hundreds, maybe thousands, of the loveliest cream-colored creatures appeared, a kaleidoscope of color flying around my car as I continued down the jungle road.

Whenever I share this, people try their best to explain it in nonspiritual terms: maybe it was the beginning of butterfly season in Mexico, or maybe the butterflies were attracted to the blue color of the car, or maybe I just dreamed it. The interesting thing is that I didn't initially see it as significant. I just thought it was strange to have all these butterflies with their almost transparent wings flying along with me.

It didn't dawn on me until later that maybe God Himself was enveloping me, affirming my journey and ordering and lighting my path.

23. A FLASHING YELLOW LIGHT AND MORE MACHINE GUNS

An hour and a half later I saw the flashing yellow light in the distance and a sign pointing to San Blas. I slowed to make the turn, and soon I was driving through the middle of a village whose road was so bad I could barely clock ten miles per hour. Toddlers played unsupervised near the road. Trash and debris were strewn everywhere except in the town square. There a Catholic church stood as if to protest the squalor all around.

This was the first of many villages I passed on the way to San Blas. All fit this description, each in a similar state of disrepair, each town square and church looking like the previous one.

After forty-five minutes I could see the ocean.

It was breathtaking, a striking contrast to the jungle road that was lined with dilapidated houses, saloons, and unfinished condos. A late-model black-and-white truck was approaching rapidly. As it got closer, I could see the light on top—a police vehicle. Eight men stood in the back, armed with small machine guns. They passed me at seventy. Once again I was aware of the potential danger I was in. No one who cared for me, no one who had the ability to get me out of this country, knew where I was. If something sinister were to happen, I might never be found.

At last I reached San Blas, another town built around a square and a Catholic church. I found my way to the Garza Canela and approached the front desk, where a woman worked quietly. Josefina. I reminded her that she was saving a room for me.

"We do have a room for tonight, but as I said on the telephone, we are booked until Monday," she said curtly. "I can call the Flamingo and see if they have anything."

"That will be fine," I said. "But right now I need you to help me."

"What do you mean?"

"I'm here to find the families of the three fishermen. I don't speak Spanish, and I need you to take me to where they live and translate for me."

She looked at me as if I had asked her to pull a rabbit out of a hat. "No," she said emphatically.

"I can't do this on my own. If you don't help me, I'm dead in the water."

"I told you," she said, "there's a large group coming in tomorrow. I can't leave the hotel. Certainly you can understand."

"What am I supposed to do, Josefina?" I thought if I said her name in the middle of my pleading, it might help.

"I am sorry," she said.

Period. Game over. I started to walk outside to get some air. A couple of years ago this would have been the pause in the action where I'd smoke several cigarettes and have a tasty little mix of antidepressants and clear liquor. Not now. As I walked toward the exit, a short Mexican man, who looked as though he could be golfer Lee Trevino's little brother, stood just inside the door, blocking the way. He seemed to be expecting me.

"When do we start?" he said in English.

"Excuse me? You speak English?"

"Yes, of course. Bakersfield. Ten years. When do we start?"

"Are you saying you can help me?"

"Sure," he said casually.

"Right now?"

"Yes, right now." He spoke as if he had been waiting for me all day.

"Let me get to my room and get cleaned up," I said. "I'll meet you in the bar in fifteen minutes." He nodded, and I rushed through check-in and headed for my room.

Looking at myself in the mirror, I saw that my beard was nearly a week old. I pulled a cheap hotel-issue razor from my bag. I had no shaving cream, so I spent the next few minutes lathering up a tiny bar of hand soap and proceeded to shave with a razor that was so dull it pulled the whiskers out of my skin. By the time I was done, I had half a dozen pieces of toilet paper on my neck and looked like Freddy Krueger.

The guy who said he could help me was waiting in the hotel bar. He told me his name was Armando Santiago, and he knew he was holding all the cards.

I leaned in close. "Armando," I said softly, "I'm here to see if I can find the fishermen…or the families of the fishermen. I've come to help them. I want to tell their story of faith, and I need you to translate and help me get around. I'll pay you. How much would you need?"

"I usually get $120 a day for taking people bird-watching," he said.

So God in His infinite wisdom to accomplish His purposes had decided to pair me, an American whose face was spotted with toilet paper, with a Mexican bird-watcher. *Sure, why not?* I agreed to Armando's rate, and he tapped his watch.

"We have to go before it gets dark, or we won't find anyone," he said impatiently.

"I know," I said. "But first I need you to understand what I'm trying to do so you can capture the emotion of what I'm saying when you translate." I showed him an e-mail exchange I'd had with Eli about how this seemed to be a story of hope and faith and asked him to look it over. He scanned the sheet of paper for all of forty-five seconds and looked up.

"Okay," he said. "I understand."

When I asked him to tell me what he understood, he wasn't even close.

Armando suggested that our best bet was to try the city's director of tourism. It didn't make much sense to me that the first place we would go was the tourism director's office. It didn't make much sense that San Blas even had one, but Armando was all I had. I handed him the keys to the Fiesta, but he refused.

"I always let someone else drive," he said. "It's much safer that way."

It didn't sound as if he meant "safer" in terms of insurance coverage. I wondered if he secretly knew that drivers of rental cars often turned up drawn and quartered in back alleys.

We drove toward the Pacific on a dirt road with potholes so deep that each time the Fiesta dropped into one, muddy water splattered the side windows.

Armando asked me to pull over in front of a run-down, salmon-colored building. The tourism office.

Once inside, we could see a pair of steel-toed boots propped up on the arm of an old sofa. The boots belonged to a sleeping man wearing camouflage and cradling a rather large machine gun. Armando had no reaction; apparently a man taking an afternoon nap with an assault weapon was a common sight. The man began to stir.

I slowly backed out into the street, both to separate myself from Armando and to reduce the risk of my body being riddled with bullets. I decided to wait in the Fiesta.

Soon Armando emerged. "The tourism director is not here," he said. "We should try city hall and look for the mayor."

Without any other explanation, Armando got back into the car. We drove to the center of town and stopped across from the church in a busy square where many old men were hanging out. We walked through the main entrance of a half-painted building and into a large courtyard. Dozens of people were there, mostly talking on cell phones. They seemed out of place with their khakis, dress shirts, and shoulder bags. Of course, I was the one out of place, the only six-foot white guy wearing a pink shirt within a few hundred miles.

The air was buzzing, as if something big was about to happen. Armando excused himself; I stayed in the courtyard. To my left was a guy waiting on a bench with an expensive-looking camera hanging from his shoulder. The logo on his tan vest said "TV Azteca." The press had arrived.

Armando peeked out of an office and signaled for me to come in.

I was introduced to the mayor of San Blas, who couldn't speak any English. He was in the middle of arranging the fishermen's return to Mexico from the Marshall Islands.

I also met Silverio, the city manager and apparently the number-two man in San Blas, although I had a feeling he was really number one. After an exchange between Armando and Silverio in Spanish, Armando informed me that Silverio had decided I was worthy to hear him speak directly in English.

Now that Silverio was speaking to me, he agreed to meet with me later that night. Apparently, he considered himself a dealmaker and someone who could speak for the fishermen.

We left the mayor's office, having learned nothing of value, and I paid Armando $120 for less than a day's worth of runaround and disappointment.

While I was unimpressed with the mayor and Silverio and doubtful of Armando's purposes in linking me up with them, these were the only connections I had. I had to follow through with what was there.

That night I made my way to the hotel lobby by nine, but Silverio didn't show. By eleven I gave up. I went back to my room, flipped on the TV, and saw that the news coverage of the fishermen had hit a new low.

As the news anchor read his copy, footage of the fishermen in Majuro appeared alongside still photos of a plane crash. They were comparing the fishermen's story to the Uruguayan rugby team whose airplane crashed in the Andes in 1972. The men who survived that crash were stranded for two months, and some of them fed on the dead bodies that had been preserved in the snow. I shut off the TV and went to bed, counting doubts instead of sheep.

This had been one of the longest days of my life.

24. What's News?

For the three fishermen trying to get home after some ten months away, the stopover in Honolulu must have seemed like slow torture.

Yet they were heroes again, greeted by another welcoming committee made up of Mexicans living on the big island. They were cheered as the "Lost Sons of Mexico," and some waved the Mexican flag as others took photographs and adorned the fishermen with traditional Hawaiian leis.

From there, the itinerary called for a quick change of planes in Los Angeles, then on to Mexico City.

There was no welcoming committee in Los Angeles. While the rescue of the fishermen was carried by media outlets in the US, their story and many others were overshadowed by another American headline that turned into a classic media circus: "John Mark Karr Arrested in Bangkok for Murder of JonBenét Ramsey." But for the fishermen, the more subdued media presence in L.A. must have been a relief. They were able to move through the LAX terminal quickly and board the plane for Mexico without much attention.

The last leg of the fishermen's journey home proved uneventful, an overnight flight scheduled to land in Mexico City around five thirty in the morning. The three slept most of the way, like most of the other passengers on the plane.

When the lights in the cabin were brightly lit upon arrival, one of the flight attendants made an announcement to the rest of the passengers that they had been flying with the three most famous men in Mexico. There was applause, and a few people took out their cell phones and cameras to snap some photos. Outside the plane, the ground crew lined the Jetway to catch a glimpse of them.

The fishermen gathered their sparse belongings and stepped off the plane. They were finally home. But Jesús, Salvador, and Lucio had no idea what lay ahead: a different breed of sharks.

25. Signs and Wonders

I sat up in bed, wide awake. It was four o'clock.

Instinctively, I grabbed my briefcase from the floor and began to rummage through it in the dark. During my many years on the road, I had often awakened at four in the morning in a hotel room and searched my briefcase for something to dull the pain. This time I was searching for my Bible, hoping to pray away my fear.

I couldn't find it. I had probably left it on the plane or at the hotel in Mexico City. So I just sat on the edge of the bed, with nothing else in the room but loneliness and anxiety. I dropped to my knees and asked God for direction.

"What do You want me to do?" I prayed in desperation. "Just show me. Whatever it is, I'll do it."

Silence, except for the chirp of the crickets.

I reached into my bag one more time, searching for an aspirin. This time I brushed a corner of something—yes, it was my Bible. It had somehow gotten tucked into an unfamiliar pocket. I pulled it out, grabbed my glasses, and let my thumb riffle its pages. I stopped, then opened it blindly to that page.

I had never played Bible roulette. I don't really recommend it, but I think God uses anything and everything. And as I sat alone in the fluorescent glow of the overhead light, God gave me a simple message of grace that didn't require confetti or a brass band.

The first words I saw were a heading in bold type: **"Pray About Everything."**

I read on: "Don't fret or worry. Instead of worrying, pray.... Put into practice what you learned from me, what you heard and saw and realized. Do that, and God, who makes everything work together, will work you into his most excellent harmonies." The verses were in Philippians, chapter 4, and they got my attention.[4]

Work me into his most excellent harmonies? I couldn't believe it. I had asked God what to do, and thirty seconds later He gave me the only possible answer. I was stunned.

Then it hit me: *I am supposed to be here!* Everything in the past seventy-two hours played back in my mind like a movie in slow motion. It all had been a prelude to this moment: Victoria's urging, Eli not being able to go to San Blas, Josefina telling me San Blas had "no hope," the "Faith" song on the radio, the first-class seat suddenly becoming available, the nudge to buy the ticket, the swarms of butterflies, Armando appearing out of nowhere... Now these verses.

I think sometimes we're so close to our own lives, so nearsighted in our own reality that we miss the obvious. At every turn when I faced a serious discouragement, something pushed me forward. Some sign, some event, some nudge.

I was under no illusion; I still thought getting to the fishermen was a long shot. But I was now driven by a divine confidence. I was convinced that something special was happening. I was supposed to be here, God was in it, and that was all I needed to know.

I also thought no one would believe it.

So I spent the next four hours recording every detail, from the day Victoria told me about the fishermen until the Philippians moment in the hotel before dawn. From that point on, I began to keep a diary of everything that occurred—every leg of the journey; every phone call, e-mail, and prayer; notes about the weather and snippets of conversations. I now believed that everything mattered.

When the sun came up, I could feel the momentum of something incredibly big.

I was at breakfast, and Armando and Silverio showed up, along with another man, Eduardo, who seemed to be Silverio's right-hand guy.

I told them all the crazy coincidences that had happened since I'd arrived in Mexico—everything. Then I read them the Bible passage that had answered my prayer.

They just stared at me.

"Gentlemen," I said, "I think I am the one who is supposed to tell this story."

26. A Different Breed of Sharks

The three fishermen had no idea what had developed overnight in the world media.

It had been learned that originally five men had been on the boat. That spread like wildfire through the media corps. As happens with most survival stories, the press speculated: had the men managed to survive by using the dead for food?

The fishermen were taken to the airport medical center and were examined before being placed in front of the media. Although they were very thin and their limbs were still swollen, they were in excellent health, according to the doctors. That diagnosis simply threw more gasoline on the media fire. How could men at sea for so long be in relatively good condition?

Having been cleared by the doctors at the Mexico City airport, the fishermen were escorted from the medical bay to a conference room filled with the press frothing at the mouth to sink their teeth into them. The doors opened...and it started.

Jesús, Salvador, and Lucio were all smiles when they entered the room. Camera lights flashed nonstop for a few minutes. The men waved and stood behind their chairs as reporters shouted over one another. The questions were undecipherable. The "amazing survival" story was quickly overtaken by a media demanding answers to wild theories and rumors of cannibalism and drug running. It was a feeding frenzy.

The men finally took their seats, each in front of a microphone. Several police officers lined the walls, watching the fishermen closely. The questions came at them like a tsunami that pushed relentlessly with boundless energy and unstoppable force. The smiles on the faces of the fishermen vanished as they slouched down in their chairs, stunned by the barrage. They seemed to be staring right through the reporters. The rapid-fire questions continued.

Like third-grade boys being forced to watch a production of *Hamlet,* the fishermen heard the words, but they could not comprehend what they were hearing. These men had never faced so many questions. They rarely faced a situation where anyone asked them a question. And the fury and antagonism in the room was shocking to them.

"That is not true," Lucio responded angrily at one point. Then he calmly spoke these words into the mike: "To people that don't believe us, well, they should hope that they never have to go through this." Finally the reporters allowed the men to answer.

"Will you take a lie-detector test?" one reporter shouted.

"Yes," Jesús replied without hesitation. "We have nothing to hide."

Several allegations robbed the fishermen of the heroic welcome they deserved. Those allegations are easily addressed, and other evidence supports the veracity of their story.

People considered it suspicious that the doctors had pronounced the fishermen to be in good medical condition when they arrived in Mexico City. Yet, in the heat of the media moment, people were not taking into account that it had been several weeks since the men's rescue, during which time they'd received medical attention, food, and rest. Indeed, they *were* in bad shape when they were picked up by the Taiwanese trawler. But two weeks on board the trawler before arriving at port and several more days in Majuro had provided some recovery time.

Of course the accusation of cannibalism was leveled at the fishermen; it's leveled at many survivors in the aftermath of a rescue. People wonder about it when they hear a survivor account, and the media often fan those flames, usually without facts or logic. But for most people in a survivor situation, such an act is so abhorrent that it would be considered a very last resort for staying alive. And whether they actually come to that last resort depends on their skills and abilities. In the case of the fishermen, the Pacific was their environment, the world they knew. They clearly had the opportunity, ability, and experience to capture food and rainwater to help sustain them.

Another suspicion was that the fishermen were drug runners. It is true that that area of the Pacific is notorious as a traffic corridor for Colombian drugs. But it is also true that such suspicions are unfairly generalized to all Mexicans in boats on the Pacific. Many Mexicans are indeed just fishermen who work hard to make a meager living by catching fish. Some simple journalistic legwork in those first days might have surfaced the truth that these guys had no history of drug running but were truly fishermen. Ultimately, no one other than the three fishermen on the boat knows what actually happened, and at some point we have to assess the veracity and character of the fishermen.

And there are greater reasons to doubt the media. Though many decry the state of American news reporting, the practices of so-called journalism in other countries are often much worse. And this sensationalistic way of shaping stories tends to be the nature of the Mexican press. They do not claim to be in the business of journalism. The companies that operate magazines and newspapers aren't considered journalism companies; rather, they call themselves "media companies" and are simply in the business of making money. The usual checks and balances of serious journalism are not in place; instead speculation and innuendo rule, making it more opinionating than reporting.

There was also the reality of the political cauldron that the fishermen were unwittingly dropped into. On July 2, five weeks before the rescue of the three fishermen, the people of Mexico voted in the presidential election. The sitting president, Vicente Fox, was ineligible to run for another term. Felipe Calderón and Andrés Manuel López Obrador were the two main contenders.

Four days later, on July 6, the Federal Electoral Institute announced that Calderón had won by less than 1 percent of the vote. His opponent claimed there were polling irregularities and declared himself the winner. It got ugly. By early August there were angry protests in the streets—up to a million people, depending on whom you believed. It was a heavyweight boxing match that had gone fifteen rounds, with each guy celebrating as if he had won and thinking that the more he acted like a winner, the better his chances were of being awarded the championship belt. Each candidate had internal polling that showed him to be the winner. It was a national crisis.

In July and early August, the media coverage of the election was extensive, with reporters waiting and hoping that the situation would explode. News stories about electoral "materials" being found in trash dumps only fueled speculation that the election had been fixed. The newspaper *Reforma* later reported that these "materials" were old photocopies that had nothing to do with the outcome. But in the media biz, a rigged election was a great story for a few weeks.

In short, the media were already cynical. They were sharks in the water looking for blood. To have a rigged election story and a drug-dealing, man-eating, survivor story going on at the same time is a dream come true for the media. These are the stories that can stretch out over weeks or months. Each makes for great two-inch headlines, higher ratings and revenues, and for some strange reason a public that is willing to consume it all in excess.

This was the world the fishermen came back to. It was the spectacle I watched on TV from not far away.

27. Going Home

I watched the Mexico City press conference from my hotel room in Tepic, the capital city of Nayarit, the state where San Blas is located.

Silverio and Eduardo had earlier invited me to fly to Mexico City so I could be there when the fishermen stepped off the plane from L.A. At the last minute the mayor of San Blas decided that he and the governor would go instead of the unknown gringo from out of town. Silverio asked me to meet him in Tepic because that was where the fishermen were supposed to fly to after Mexico City.

So I had driven to Tepic alone, checked into a hotel that afternoon, and met with Silverio, who laid out the fishermen's itinerary and gave me one of his cell phones so I could contact him easily. Unfortunately, it had no minutes left on it. While I was out buying more minutes, I bought a white linen suit, thinking that when I finally met the men, I should look professional. Maybe I thought white would be a persuasive color, even angelic. Well, it seemed like a good idea at the time. (I never wore it.)

Eli watched the press conference in Mexico City and translated everything for me by speakerphone. It was like watching a football game with the volume turned down on the television but your favorite radio announcer giving the play-by-play. The Mexican TV networks were doing wall-to-wall coverage. (What I didn't know was that the American networks were also in wall-to-wall coverage, but on the extradition of JonBenét Ramsey's alleged killer.)

What I saw on TV was extraordinary. Camera flashes lit up the room. Initially there was applause and then a few cheers. It was as if the tres pescadores were the first Mexican astronauts to reach the moon. For a moment it seemed like a grand celebration, but then everything quickly went south.

"What happened?" I shouted at the speakerphone.

"They just asked them if they killed the other two guys," Eli answered.

"What are the fishermen saying?" I yelled.

"One of them just said that it's not true and that they have nothing to hide," said Eli. "And just now a reporter asked if they would take a lie-detector test."

"What did they say?"

"Yes," Eli announced.

My mind was racing. Were these penniless, uneducated, unsophisticated fishermen capable of anything so grand as a conspiracy? It seemed as though the media had talked themselves into believing that the most evil possibilities were true. As I watched and listened to these men being labeled guilty, I was more determined than ever to meet them and hear their story firsthand.

After the press conference Silverio called and asked me to come to the Tepic airport. I was hopeful now that I was about to actually meet the fishermen.

Earlier, I had called my attorney in the US to have her hire a Mexican lawyer for me. If I could talk with the fishermen and convince them I was, like them, a man of faith, and I was the one who could best tell their story, then I'd need someone there to witness whatever agreement might be reached. All that I would be doing had to be transparent and disclosed properly in case anyone was expecting something less than honorable. I wasn't the guy for that.

I sped to the airport and found Silverio in the thick of running things.

He introduced me to a governor's aide and some reporters. We were talking when a throng of people walked in. It was, seemingly, a family and apparently the extended family as well. It turned out they were the family of Lucio.

Soon enough I was able to meet them all: Lucio's mother, father, brothers, and sisters, as well as his nieces, nephews, uncles, aunts, and grandmother, Panchita. At least four generations were present.

Panchita, in her eighties, was the matriarch of the tribe and the unquestionable leader and moral authority of the family. I noticed how each family member treated her with respect. She reminded me of my mom, so loved by her children, grandchildren, and great-grandchildren. Like my mother, she had obviously been through a lot. Even before I met her, Panchita's presence was a calming force.

These were strange moments, awkward and intense. It was noisy one minute and eerily silent the next. I was nervous and excited for my own reasons, and family members were understandably filled with anticipation, but there was nothing for them to do, and of course, they really didn't know me or what I was doing there.

I tried to connect with them with my eyes, a handshake, and a simple *"Hola."* But I didn't get much response. To them, I was just one more peculiar occurrence in the crazy world that held their son who was once dead.

The children were the only ones making noise; they ran around and played loudly, as kids do. I'm sure they didn't know the significance of the moment, just that they were in a strange place and something exciting was happening. I'm not sure they even knew or remembered who Lucio was. When you're a little kid with eight uncles on each side of the family, I suppose it gets hard to distinguish the ones who live next door from the ones who get lost at sea for nine months.

In the middle of the kids' commotion, the adult members of Lucio's family were subdued. I couldn't tell if their silence was caused by simple weariness from years of a fishing life or if they were in some level of shock at what was happening. Perhaps both. They, too, were out of place, out of their world, here at the airport. It was a strange day.

But, miraculously, their beloved Lucio was coming home to them.

I looked around and noticed that something was missing. "Where are Jesús's and Salvador's families?" I asked the aide.

Then he dropped the bomb on me. "Oh, they aren't from here," he said. "They're being flown back to the cities they're from. I'm sorry no one told you."

28. Electric Connections

Getting close to the fishermen now wouldn't be just one grand encounter but apparently was going to require three separate pursuits to approach each one individually and convince him of my vision and purpose. *Sigh*. It's great to have God's nudges and nods along the journey, but that's no guarantee the journey will be easy.

Lucio's plane circled the Tepic airport once and came in for a landing. A crowd of family members, the bishop, and the governor's men stood on the tarmac about seventy-five yards from where the plane stopped. Hundreds of others watched from behind a fence, including a fifteen-piece marching band and many media people.

The cabin door opened, and passengers started filing out. A few dozen people walked down the stairs. Then no one came out. Everyone waited in silence. Eventually, the mayor of San Blas stepped out of the plane, then the governor. It wasn't completely choreographed, but it had a brilliant, crisp, dramatic feel to it.

And then Lucio appeared at the door of the plane. His head ducked through the small opening, and the band started playing, the crowd cheered, and the family let out a collective gasp.

Lucio slowly came down the four or five steps and started walking toward the crowd of relatives. When he got within twenty paces, his mother burst into tears. Lucio picked up his pace to a jog.

The scene was electric. The family was silent, overcome with emotion, but everyone else was buzzing and cheering. It was controlled chaos until Lucio reached his mother, and then the floodgates opened. Tears of joy.

All were witnesses to a man resurrected, back from the dead.

I'm not sure I knew how I had actually managed to get into that time and place. And, again, I really didn't know what I was doing there. My spiritual quest couldn't be explained logically. This scene was improbable to say the least and, by any definition, divinely arranged.

The tarmac crowd numbered in the hundreds—in that moment one big happy family. It was surreal, and I looked incredibly out of place. I was one of just a few people there who spoke English.

I had never before seen unbridled elation like that from adults. It was child-like joy from the family and unrestrained expressions of love from friends and people of his church whose simple faith swallowed up the antagonism of the media.

Suddenly I was part of a swarm of people closing in on Lucio, circling him. I saw Silverio attempting to guide the friendly mob, with Lucio at the very center, toward an exit into the parking lot. I pitched in.

There was a moment in the chaos when Lucio looked at me. Our eyes locked. It was only seconds, but it felt much longer. Something in him pulled me deeper into what he had experienced. I felt a sadness in his spirit. A brokenness. It surprised me because it was so distinct from the exhilaration and joy bubbling up in the people around him.

Later I would learn that Lucio's pain had nothing to do with his time at sea. It was an emptiness he felt from a difficult relationship with his father and mother. Maybe he saw the same thing in my eyes. Perhaps he could connect with the sad desire in my heart: a longing for a father who loved me.

The final legs of the fishermen's journeys home were the first time they'd been separated in eleven months.

I would learn later that, upon landing in his home state of Sinaloa, Jesús was also given a hero's welcome. Hundreds of people showed up, holding signs above their heads or carrying children on their shoulders to catch a glimpse of him as they shouted and cheered. Jesús wrapped his arms around his brother for the first time in nearly a year.

When he got to his village of Las Arenitas, he gave an adoring embrace to his young wife, Jocelyn, who had been ripped to pieces, believing that she had lost her husband and that she would be raising their young son and four-month-old baby girl by herself.

He met his daughter, Juliana, for the first time.

Jesús wept.

A gigantic Fourth of July–type celebration ensued, complete with fireworks: a brightly lit and sparkling cross, a fifty-foot-tall swirling wheel with multiple explosions, and hundreds of surface-to-air-missile-type fireworks skyrocketing into the carnival-like atmosphere.

Going home was different for Salvador. He flew to Oaxaca, in south central Mexico. He was met with virtually no fanfare and with an uncomfortable silence from sisters he hadn't seen in years. Government officials assumed he would prefer to fly to the area he was originally from. But they figured wrong; Salvador had long forgotten about his life there. Few people there knew him.

He was a celebrity nonetheless, so a small celebration was held in his honor, and a few bottle rockets were lit at the end. The once-obscure day laborer and fisherman was, for a moment, the most famous man in town, even if no one celebrating actually knew him.

29. Middlemen

Within twenty-four hours everything came crashing down. The attorney I'd hired found me. I quickly learned he hadn't graduated from law school yet. Basically, he was just a hundred-dollar-an-hour translator. A nice kid, though.

That night Lucio, his family, and friends partied at a nearby motel. I asked Silverio for some time with Lucio. I wanted to explain my vision for their story, and I also had ideas about how he and the others should respond to the charges the press was making. (I'd picked up a few things during my time in and around Hollywood; I knew something about celebrities handling the media.)

I also wanted Lucio to know that I was not one of those Hollywood guys who makes a deal for the rights to the story, then creates whatever movie he thinks will sell the most tickets. I wanted to portray the truth of their ordeal, the reality of their lives, and the faith that ultimately had rescued them. I just wanted a chance to tell them that.

I was also secretly hoping for an opportunity for a few personal words with Lucio about what he'd gone through, not only on the Pacific, but also in life. I didn't know if he could understand how I, too, had been adrift and hopeless. I wondered if he had seen in my eyes what I had seen in his.

Silverio agreed to set up a meeting with Lucio the next day. Lunch at Hotel Casa Mañana.

Silverio had not asked for money yet, which was encouraging, even though I did offer to compensate him for his help. Meanwhile, the meter on the kid attorney was running 24/7. He was going to be by my side for several days at $2,400 a day, plus expenses.

I could hear a sucking noise coming from my 401(k).

When I arrived twenty-four hours later at the restaurant, Silverio was waiting with Eduardo. Apparently, they were now Lucio's handlers. It had come to this: a hard negotiation right up front just to get five minutes with Lucio.

"Well, you know," Eduardo said slowly, "there are other offers."

I had negotiated thousands of deals in my days with the studios. I had learned from the best the business had ever seen. We operated on a "less is more" strategy most of the time. The less information you give away, the more strength you have in your negotiating position. It keeps everyone guessing. The very last thing I would ever do is discuss, or even mention, anything about other interested parties. If I did allude to the competiveness of a negotiation, it was going to be at the very last second as the window was closing to make a final and best offer... You know, *going, going, gone.*

I certainly wasn't trying to drive an unfair bargain with the fishermen. Their story was worth something, and it was an opportunity for them to lead easier lives. I actually wanted them to do well—however my attempt played out. What concerned me were the guys between me and them—these handlers. I didn't trust that any agreement struck would fully trickle down to the fishermen themselves. Old Joe's skills were at my fingertips, and I knew I might have to play a little hardball.

Eduardo's opening salvo about other offers told me a lot. I suspected there probably weren't any. I decided to call their bluff: "You know what, guys? I'm done. I'm on the next plane out of here. Thanks, but I've had enough."

I told them that if they really had other offers, they should take one of them because the press was already calling the fishermen drug dealers, murderers, and cannibals. Their story was going to be written with or without them, and the truth would run a poor second to whatever sold the most newspapers.

I slid my proposal across the table. "Here's my offer. You know how to find me."

I stood to leave. "Do me a favor," I said, "and do the fishermen a favor. Take an offer. Anyone's offer."

Then I walked away. I packed my bags and took the first flight out.

30. No. Maybe. Yes.

Carmen picked me up at the Atlanta airport. There was much she didn't know about the events of my trip. Frankly, we'd had very little communication during my ten days away; circumstances often made it impossible for me to call. Moreover, she had no idea of all that was going on inside me.

When we got into the car, I could see she was anxious. It had been hard for her to hold down the fort for so long.

"So?" she asked softly. It was a question she had every right to ask.

"I never got to meet the fishermen," I said. I couldn't bear to look at her.

"How much money did you spend on this trip?" she asked. There was no hint of anger in her voice, just real concern, which only made me feel worse.

"I don't know, and I don't want to know."

We didn't speak for the rest of the trip home.

The next day at the office I was greeted by my colleagues with the silent treatment.

I tried to explain. "This is a story of epic proportions that could inspire millions of people," I said, believing my own words even if no one else did. "I feel called to do this. I think God has big plans for—"

"It doesn't fit our model," said one of the partners. He echoed what I had heard before I had left. He was right about that, and I knew it. *But what about all the things that had happened on this trip?* I asked myself. *Were they just a string of coincidences?*

It seemed as though the whole project was over and that I'd suckered myself into a wild-goose chase. I started in on myself: *My wife thinks I've gone off the deep end. My partners want me out. I will have no income again, and I've already drained a big chunk of my 401(k) with my summer of Joe.*

I was crushed. *How could I be such an idiot?*

Carmen was, once again, gentle with me. She knew how disappointed I was, and while she certainly had a right to, she didn't rub it in my face. She let me be as I moped around the house. A lot of grass would have to be cut to build my confidence back up.

A few nights later I heard from Armando. Yeah, the guy who showed up out of nowhere to be one of my angels. Once again he just came out of no-where, this time in the form of an e-mail asking me to call him. He said he was with two of the fishermen, Jesús and Salvador.

I called him right away and asked what the men thought of my offer. He said they had never heard anything about it. I told Armando that if he could get them to meet with me, I would be on the next plane to Mexico. He said he would work on it.

I considered it a long shot, but I wanted to be ready just in case.

That next week I had planned to be in Colorado for a men's expedition with a group called Adventures of the Heart. I would embark on a mission of guy stuff with twenty-four brothers at Redcloud Ranch, digging deep inside ourselves to discover who we really are. I had a magnificent and loving wife and two beautiful and gifted daughters, who all loved me, and they deserved nothing less. If things were going to be different for future generations, it was up to me to change.

I knew I had not always been the best husband and father I could be, but I was determined to be better than I had ever been. I wanted to continue undoing the damage from my relationship with my father. I didn't know it at the time, but this study of my experiences would be instrumental in healing the cruelty, the physical and emotional abuse, and the shame of my childhood. Perhaps then I could start becoming the father that God created me to be and not repeat the history of my family passed down generation after generation.

I called the leader of the expedition, Reese, a pastor and a friend, leaving him the message that there was a chance I'd have to skip the Colorado retreat because I might have to go back to Mexico.

He called back the next day. "Joe," he said, "go back to Mexico if you really think you need to, but if this is something God wants you to be part of, then you will be, and there's not much you can do about it. If He doesn't want you to be part of something, then you won't be, and there isn't a thing you can do about that either. If it's meant for you, it will be there when you get back from Colorado."

I believed him. His advice was the beginning of a new understanding for me: trusting God with outcomes. So I left home for another week but flew to Colorado, which turned out to be the right move. I got to share all the stuff that had happened to me in Mexico, and I got a chance to be in God's country, listening to Him every day among the majestic mountains He created.

While I was there, Reese gave me another piece of good advice. "If you're going to live in God's kingdom," he said, "it's going to take every ounce of passion and forcefulness you've got. Things are going to get fierce. That's why you were given a fierce heart." Then he looked me straight in the eye and said, "Do you have anything better to do with your life?"

Duh!

On the final day of the retreat, Reese gave us a photocopy of a prayer of protection and suggested we start every day with it:

> Father, thank you for your angels. I summon them in the
> authority of Jesus Christ and release them to war for me and
> my household and my life and in my sphere of influence.
> Thank you for those who pray for me. I know full well I need
> these prayers. I ask you to send forth your Spirit and raise these
> men and women up, arouse them, unite them, establish and
> direct them, raising up numerous prayers and intercessions for
> me. I call forth the Kingdom of the Lord Jesus Christ this day
> throughout my home, my family, my life, and all areas of my
> influence. All this I pray in the name of Jesus Christ, with all
> glory and honor and thanks to Him.

That very afternoon I received word from Silverio that the fishermen were ready to meet with me on Tuesday morning at the Hotel Casa Mañana.

31. Nudges

Tuesday was around the corner, and I decided that instead of flying back to Atlanta, it would make more sense to fly directly to Mexico. Once again Carmen handled this news with grace.

Three of the guys on the expedition said they were going to leave early for the Denver airport and asked if anyone needed a lift. I was busting at the seams to get back to Mexico, and going to an airport as soon as possible would get me one step closer, so I jumped at the chance.

We piled into the car at 4:30 a.m. for a six-hour drive to the airport, and a guy named Lee drove while I copiloted. Somewhere between Gunnison and Denver, Lee asked me a question. "I heard bits and pieces of things—your childhood, a transformation, the fishermen, and Mexico. Can you start at the beginning and tell me your story?"

Up to this point I had told my personal story only a few times, and I hadn't really discussed with anyone the details of what had happened just days earlier in Mexico. So I went ahead and told him everything, the whole kit and caboodle. As I talked, the other two, who'd been snoring the miles away in the backseat, awakened and listened too. Three hours later I finished. They were stunned. *I* was stunned. It wasn't just the childhood stuff, or the career in Hollywood, or the struggle through addiction and depression, or the story of the fishermen, or my recent experiences with God.

It was all of it.

When we parted ways at the Denver airport, we exchanged contact information. One of the guys asked if I would share the story at his church. I gladly accepted.

I was able to convert my return ticket to Atlanta for value toward a ticket to Mexico, and I called Eli and the kid lawyer, asking them to meet me in San Blas at the Casa Mañana.

On the flight to Mexico, I started thinking about how wonderful—and astonishing—this whole thing had become. I wondered what must be going through Carmen's mind about this on-again, off-again, on-again undertaking. *He is completely nuts!* It really was the only logical conclusion she could come to. *Right?*

I quickly put together a simple PowerPoint presentation (that's right, a PowerPoint, in English no less). I was prepared, at last, to meet with the three fishermen. If indeed this was really going to happen.

I still had my doubts.

When the doors of the meeting room opened, my Mexican "team"—Silverio, Eduardo, and Armando—and just one of the fishermen, Salvador, walked in with an entourage of friends, city officials, and the parish priest. I had flown in the kid attorney to be a witness and Eli to translate.

Even though I couldn't understand the Spanish, I was surprised to hear an aggressive tone coming from Salvador's posse.

"Eli, what's going on?" I asked.

"They're talking about how they aren't getting enough," he said in between all the chatter.

What? "Please ask them to stop," I said to Eli.

He raised his hands in the international sign of "calm down," which they did.

"Eli, please ask them to give me just a few minutes to explain how I got here...and why I am here." Eli quickly had their attention with the translation. Everyone took a seat around a block of tables set up in a U shape.

"Tell them if they don't like what I have to say, then we'll pack up and never bother them again." This seemed to put them more at ease as they nodded, giving me the go-ahead.

I started talking, and Eli translated my entire story with all the twists and turns. I could tell he was explaining it to them perfectly. He relayed my entire journey: My Hollywood experience with the studio. The moment Victoria told me about their story. The inexplicable tug it had on my heart that caused me to risk everything to come and find them. The vision I had for a story of faith that could inspire millions of people. All the "coincidences" I had experienced while on this mysterious quest.

Thirty minutes into the story, Padre Pedro, an eighty-year-old priest, stood up and began to speak directly to Salvador.

I leaned over and whispered to Eli, "What's he saying?"

"He has just given his blessing," Eli conveyed. "He says he can see the kind of men we are, that we are men of God. That this is divine providence."

After the padre's comments, Salvador said yes.

I had been wondering why Lucio wasn't at this meeting. He was the only one of the three who was really from the area. Turned out, it was because no one could find him. He had been gone for about a week. It seems he had a pattern of disappearing for several days at a time. I probably would too if I lived where he lives. I suggested we go to his house, about an hour away, and look for him. Eli and the kid attorney went back to Mexico City.

Salvador, Eduardo, and a couple of others piled into my car. We headed to Lucio's grandmother's house, which is where he lived, along with six of his uncles. But he wasn't there.

Then we tried another uncle's house. Again Lucio wasn't there, but this uncle, Remigio, was. Uncle Remigio was in his midforties, with speckled gray hair and a speaking voice that sounded as though he were singing. He greeted me with a handshake, while wearing just pants. No shirt. No shoes. Just pants. He and I are roughly the same age, but he looked sixty. His hands and feet were rough and worn like a seasoned catcher's mitt.

So I went through my PowerPoint presentation for a shirtless, shoeless man as several other people (I suspected relatives of Lucio) looked on. I doubt they understood any of it. Afterward, I closed my computer and asked my audience, with the help of Eduardo, "Where is Lucio?" His uncle was the only one to answer, shrugging his shoulders. He had no idea.

Just then I recognized Lucio as he came strolling up the path.

He had a huge smile on his face and seemed delighted to see Salvador. He didn't recognize me from the craziness at the Tepic airport. I'm sure everything he'd experienced since stepping back on land had been veiled in fog.

I did a shortened version of the presentation again, asking when I was done what Lucio thought of it. Salvador said something in Spanish to Lucio. Lucio said something in Spanish to his uncle, who nodded. Lucio looked at me, smiled, and gave me the "okay" sign and a nod.

That was all I needed. Salvador and Lucio were on board. It was really happening. Now all I had to do was find Jesús.

Fortunately, someone had a piece of paper that had a phone number for Jesús. Lucio's aunt disappeared into their hut and came back with a telephone in her hand, unwound the wire, and plugged it into a jack outside. She dialed and handed the phone to Salvador, who repeated to Eduardo everything he was hearing from the other end of the line.

After a brief exchange with Eduardo, I found out that Jesús didn't want to be bothered. The governor of his state was coming to see him next week.

Next week? I just needed thirty minutes with the guy. I couldn't imagine that he was tied up nonstop between now and then, unless he had hired a publicist and booked Oprah, Dave, and Jay, with Regis and Kelly on the side.

I had to use a little muscle. I told Eduardo to tell Salvador to tell Jesús that I couldn't wait, that I would go wherever he was, but it had to be by tomorrow. Jesús finally agreed. We would meet at ten the next morning in front of the cathedral in Mazatlán, about six hours north through the jungle.

It was already five in the evening. In case there were problems, I didn't want to wait until morning to leave. I asked Eduardo to translate to the others that I would like to drive to Mazatlán that evening. I got quizzical stares. They considered the trip to be treacherous in the dark. Eduardo flat out said they were not going to drive there at this hour. "Too dangerous."

But I couldn't take a chance on missing Jesús, so I decided to risk driving there at night.

I asked Eduardo if he would drive Lucio and Salvador early the next morning. Eduardo drove a 1972 blue Chevy van that had rusted-out honeycomb rims, a badly airbrushed exterior, a blue velvet interior, and no air conditioning. I fondly referred to it as the Scooby-Doo Mystery Machine. I gave Eduardo two thousand pesos for food and gas, and I hoped for the best.

So it was within the hour I found myself driving through the Mexican jungle, this time at night, again without a map. My only directions: "Follow the road to Tepic until it ends, then turn left for the next five hours." Apart from a handful of people in San Blas, no one knew where I was. If I somehow ended up in one of these ravines in the jungle, I would never be found.

Amazingly, I made it with no major issues.

It was about one o'clock in the morning when I arrived, and I was exhausted. I pulled up to a taxi stand and asked where I could find the best hotel in town. Mazatlán is a resort destination, and I was ready for a good bed. Several of the drivers pointed to the building where their cabs were parked. I was so tired I had to trust them. I got a room at the Pueblo Bonita and slept better than I had in weeks.

I awoke around seven; put on a T-shirt, a pair of shorts, and flip-flops; grabbed my Bible; and headed downstairs, past the pool to the café to get a cup of coffee. The hotel employees buzzed around the property in their khaki shorts, flower-print shirts, and sneakers, cleaning everything in sight. I sometimes joke that people in Mexico clean the dirt, but it's true. I can't tell you how many times I've watched a woman hunched over a dirt path, sweeping and getting the dirt as clean as she can.

Throughout this entire crazy adventure, I had been treated kindly by almost everyone I had met in Mexico, and in that moment I was very grateful. I stepped down to the beach, grabbed a chair, and sank into it. I had tucked the prayer from my Colorado trip into my Bible, and I read it aloud. When I finished, I bowed my head again, feeling the need for something more. This was it. The Big Day. The first time I would be with all three of the fishermen in one place.

The stakes were high, and doubt quickly began to creep in. I had seen what I thought were amazing signs over the last few weeks. I felt as if each one was meant to reveal to me that I was on the right path. But today my faith was shaky, and I needed one more nod of approval. So I prayed, *Okay, God, You've proven so much to me in the last few weeks, and it seems this is where You've been leading me. If this is really what You want me to do, then I'll commit to it with every-thing I have. But, God, I need You to confirm things with me one more time.*

I was hoping for a cross lit up on the mountaintop or a lightning bolt coming out of a clear blue sky or a parting of the sea—you know, a confirmation of biblical proportions that I wasn't crazy. But when I looked up, there was no cross, no lightning bolt, and no dividing of the waters. I sat there feeling a bit silly. Maybe I had asked for one sign too many. Perhaps God was sitting on His throne in heaven, rolling His eyes. Maybe He'd had it with me. Maybe He was throwing up His hands and saying, "Enough already!"

Oh, what an idiot I was. I was asking the Alpha and the Omega for signs on *my* terms. I started laughing at the absurdity of it. I had come so far and had so many nods from God that this was right, and yet I was demanding still one more confirmation from Him to bolster my weak faith. Feeling foolish, I walked up the stairs from the beach and headed to my room to prepare for my meeting with the fishermen.

Then I felt it. Another nudge.

It was like a voice but not an audible one. The prompting whispered, *Go back over there, and ask that guy his name.* On the deck, twenty yards in the opposite direction, I saw one of the resort staff with his back to me, setting up umbrellas by the pool. I did an about-face and walked right toward him. When I got within three feet, I stopped. He had no idea I was behind him.

"*¿Cómo se llama?*" I asked. It hit me even before he started to turn around. I knew what was about to happen. First, I knew that God was laughing at me for trying to get Him to do things my way, and, second, I had a sensation I can only describe as electric and otherworldly. I could see it as clear as if I were already looking at it. I knew what his name was before he turned around—*Jesús.*

I heard him say the word at the same moment his nametag came into view. I was just starting to learn that God rarely does things the way I expect. He does things His way, sometimes in grand, sweeping gestures and other times in subtle whispers. Jesús was the only fisherman I had yet to meet, and I had become apprehensive about that happening.

Here was another Jesús, standing along my path at my precise moment of greatest doubt.

32. Trust

W“hat happened next is a blur.

I drove downtown for my meeting with the three fishermen and parked a few blocks off the main square. I took a seat on a bench across from the cathedral, giddy with expectation. It was about nine fifteen, and Jesús, the third fisherman, was due to arrive at ten. I spent the time teetering between hope and disappointment. I would later learn that Jesús was never on time, a piece of information that would have been helpful to have. I was going out of my mind.

The clock passed eleven, and then it was eleven thirty, and still no sign of Jesús. My heart sank. I worried that maybe I had missed him, that maybe he had already come and gone. I walked around the square, peeking in a few of the shops. A dozen scenarios went through my mind: *What if Jesús is the lone holdout and I am able to sign only two of the fishermen?* I chewed on that unsavory morsel for a while and then moved on to wondering about Eduardo: *Why isn't he here? What if he's led Salvador and Lucio to someone else? What if there really was another offer?* I worked over every possibility in my head and went back to my bench.

At twelve fifteen in the afternoon, two guys crossed the street and headed toward me.

Yes, indeed! It was Jesús! I jumped off the bench, so relieved that I stuttered his name as they walked past me. Jesús turned around and smiled.

"Hola, Jesús, *mi amigo,*" I said. "*Me llamo* Joe."

He looked surprised that I was speaking Spanish. *I* was surprised that I was speaking Spanish! I approached him with an outstretched arm, and he reached out and shook my hand eagerly, launching into rapid-fire dialogue in Spanish. Since I had opened in Spanish, he thought I could speak the language. I tried to follow along, feebly, and I think he may have introduced his friend, whose name I didn't catch.

I asked Jesús if he was hungry, nodding in the direction of the pizza place. I'm not sure if they understood, so I started walking toward the restaurant, and they followed. I kept my eyes peeled for Eduardo and the rest of the gang, but there was no sign of them. This was the first of many times I would want to smack Eduardo, but he was my translator, and I needed him. I motioned for Jesús and his friend to order while I fired up my laptop and dove into my presentation. Despite my limited Spanish, I thought I was doing a good job because Jesús seemed interested and nodded occasionally. (I later learned that in the Mexican culture nodding occasionally can also indicate that a person has no idea what you're talking about.) Jesús was just being polite.

When I got to the part about money, though, Jesús carefully pored over the numbers. I half expected him to pull out a green eyeshade, as if he worked for a big accounting firm. Apparently, he was fluent in the universal language of "How much is this worth to me?" He looked up from the paper with the numbers and said, "*Mas.*" The fisherman with the grade-school education was already negotiating for more.

"Maybe," I said, hedging my bet. "It could be more; it could be less." He looked at the numbers again and mumbled something that I took to mean, "Is this amount just for me?"

"No," I said. "This is for tres pescadores, not *uno* pescador." He shook his head violently, which I took to mean that this was not acceptable.

Their pizza arrived just in time. I excused myself and went to look for Eduardo. I found him and the others wandering around the square, sweating as though they had just gotten out of a sauna, or the Scooby-Doo van. I ushered them inside and motioned for them to order. They weren't interested in eating; they just wanted to talk to Jesús.

This would be the second time I wanted to smack Eduardo. He started speaking to Jesús. I had spent weeks trying to get these guys together in the same room, and Eduardo all of a sudden decided that he held all the cards. He ripped into Jesús in Spanish, ignoring my requests for a translation. All I could do was watch as Jesús became angry, raising his voice, and saying no to something that, of course, I couldn't understand because Eduardo was not translating. In fact, Eduardo was brushing me off as if I were a nuisance.

I was ready to tear my hair out. *After all this, Eduardo is sabotaging me?*

Salvador and Lucio seemed bewildered for a few moments. Then everyone at the table started yelling at each other right there in the Mexican pizza place, while I sat with my mouth hanging open, watching everything crumble before my eyes.

"What is going on here?" I said in my best I-mean-business voice.

"Jesús wants to have a lawyer look at the contracts," Eduardo shot back, "and I told him that he has to sign now."

"You're not a lawyer," I said, exasperated, "and you're not my negotiator. The only thing you should be doing right now is translating. Nothing more."

"I know how to handle these guys," he insisted.

"He doesn't have to sign anything right now," I said firmly. "Of course he can have a lawyer look at this."

I dialed Eli in Mexico City, in part because I knew he would be able to sort this out, but mostly because I needed something to do with my hands other than smack Eduardo.

"Eli, I need your help here. Jesús is about to punch Eduardo, and so am I. He's telling Jesús he has to sign this document right now. Please talk to him." I tried to hand the phone to Jesús, but he refused.

"Eli," I said, "he won't take the phone."

"Joe, he won't talk to me because he doesn't know me. Let me talk to one of the others."

I wasn't about to give the phone to Eduardo, so I gave the phone to David, a friend of Salvador's who had come with him. David and Eli had a brief conversation, and then David talked with the other men at the table. Suddenly everyone was nodding amiably. David handed the phone back to me.

"What just happened?" I asked Eli.

"They've agreed to let us tell their story, pending a lawyer looking over the document. They will sign a letter of intent today."

I was relieved but also keenly aware that if something could still go wrong, it probably would. I needed to carefully manage the process in the next few hours.

Since only Jesús and his friend had eaten, I invited everyone for lunch. I wanted to take them somewhere peaceful and nice, perhaps an establishment with tablecloths and linen napkins. I hoped we could all talk quietly, even personally, and I wanted to keep everyone together while a letter of intent was prepared for them to sign.

I asked Eduardo if he knew of such a restaurant. Eduardo said he was very familiar with Mazatlán and knew of a place in the Sands Hotel that would be perfect—on the beach.

We piled into two vehicles, my rental car and the Scooby-Doo van. When we walked into the restaurant at one thirty in the afternoon, a woman was dancing on a table, and the music was so loud you couldn't hear the person next to you if he were screaming at the top of his lungs.

Eduardo had taken us to Señor Frog's.

"This is the place you pick for us to sit down and talk?" I shouted to Eduardo. "You actually think this is appropriate?"

He shrugged.

Note to self: never let a guy driving a Scooby-Doo van pick the restaurant.

We all got back in our cars and drove to a restaurant at the Saba Hotel that was cool and quiet. Everyone ordered, and I stepped outside to call the law firm and check on the paperwork. It was done. The documents were e-mailed to me, and I had the hotel clerk print copies for everyone to sign.

Finally, around the table, one by one, the three fishermen signed the document.

I was exhilarated. I was exhausted. I thought of the frenzied weeks of searching and coming up empty handed, the days I had wasted spinning my wheels and waiting for people who never showed up, the money I'd spent that I didn't have, the times I felt completely alone and scared and drowned my sorrows in chips and salsa.

I was thrilled to finally get the fishermen's story, but I knew in my heart that the truly important thing was the incredible journey God had led me on, teaching me at each and every step how to trust Him.

33. His Plans

I could plan a course of action, but I knew that I didn't get to determine all the steps. As they say, if you want to make God laugh, tell Him your plans.

My idea was simple: put out the word and wait for the offers to come pouring in. I got in touch with a friend at *Variety*, a daily magazine that reports the wheelings and dealings of Hollywood. He had already read some information that had been leaked to the media, namely an article in which Silverio, speaking out of turn, told the media that I had paid as much as $4 million for the rights to the fishermen's story. That wasn't true, but once something like that gets into print, even in an obscure Mexican newspaper, you might as well forget about trying to set the record straight.

When I told this to my friend at *Variety*, he instantly launched into a bigger-than-a-breadbasket-but-smaller-than-a-school-bus thing—"Less than $4 million but bigger than $3 million?" *Sigh.* Eventually I was able to divert the money questions and finish the interview.

It wasn't long before the phone started ringing. Reporters, filmmakers, writers, agents, and even a few friends called when they saw the article. It gave me a boost to know that there was interest in the story. Perhaps I wasn't so crazy after all. I sifted through each message and focused on the media inquiries, particularly the magazines, since the story had been largely missed by American broadcast media. They generally don't admit mistakes, and they don't spend much time covering stories they initially missed because they were off covering some story that wasn't really a story.

It was nice to hear from some old friends. It had been a few years since I'd worked in TV, and I'd lost touch with many of my industry colleagues. In recent years no one had contacted me because I couldn't do anything for them. That's how it works. The media business is not filled with a lot of real friendships. It is very much a "What can you do for me?" kind of industry. I'm not judging; that is just the way it is. There was a time when you could do a deal on a napkin and a handshake was as good as a contract.

When I first met the fishermen, I greeted each one with a handshake. But at the end of those meetings, I gave them hugs. They didn't know what to do with that. They had not met any American men before me, so it was all new to them. Consequently, my hugs were met with an uncomfortable frozenness. They were probably shocked that another man, especially one they didn't know well, would invade their personal space like that.

As a result, there was no return hug, which is such a strange feeling for the hugger, much like a limp handshake. It's just not right. It makes you not want to hug anymore. But as strange as it felt, I kept on hugging them each time I saw them—a greeting hug and a good-bye hug. And they kept on *not* hugging back. Which was fine. I understood it wasn't part of their culture.

We had known each other for a few days when I hired a crew. We filmed each fisherman telling the story as he saw it. I sat in the background as Eli and the crew asked questions and prompted each man for as much of the story as we could get. Eli was great about relating the astonishing details to me as they came out. Each man relayed the story through the lens of his experiences—a lens that was fashioned by who he was, how he was raised, what his life had been like, and what this experience had done to him.

Jesús often ended a piece of his narrative with something humorous. There was something universal about the way he delivered the information that allowed you to understand the emotion of it all even without understanding the Spanish. He could engage you even though you had no clue what he was saying. I grew to love this about him. He and I have had hour-long conversations without really understanding a word the other was saying.

During one of these sessions, he sat with his baseball cap on backward, telling detail after detail, as he lounged on the breezy deck of a Mazatlán hotel with the turquoise-blue Pacific Ocean in the background. He spoke using his eyes, the volume of his voice, his facial muscles, his hands, and his entire body. He was verbalizing some of this detail for the first time. I could see and feel him reliving it all, being on the boat again. The words soon flowed into a cadence that gave us an uncanny understanding of what had happened, even though I was getting the translation from Eli. It was poetic. Jesús would remove his hat and push his hair back with his other hand, then put the hat back on as words fired out of his mouth at machine-gun speed. He moved from laughter to seriousness in a split second, and then back again to laughter.

In one of those rapidly shifting moments, his voice started to crack. His eyes looked down at the deck. His sentences started to trail off at the end. He flipped the bill around to the front and pulled it over his eyes. I could feel his discomfort even though I couldn't understand the language.

My heart swelled in empathy for his uneasiness.

He paused and looked off into the distance, gathering strength to continue. I knew what he was talking about; I didn't have to understand a single word. Tears streamed down his face. He sighed with big deep breaths to try to gain his composure. He took off his hat and rubbed his eyes while the hat covered his face. Jesús didn't want us to see him crying.

Eli confirmed what it was about: the death of Señor Juan.

The crew stopped filming, and Jesús got up and walked toward me. I stood up and put my hand on his shoulder and patted it gently.

"Hey...it's okay," I said softly. He nodded as if he completely understood my sympathetic eyes. I put my arms around him and hugged him.

Jesús hugged me back for the first time.

We connected. Not because we understood each other's language. Not because we understood each other's life experiences. Jesús's spirit and my spirit—and the *Holy* Spirit— connected. We connected on a heart level. We connected because we are the same. We understood each other because we are the same. His transformation and my transformation are the same.

He was stranded in an ordeal on the Pacific and came back a new man. I was stranded in my own desperate pursuits and came through them a new man. Over nine months of torturous self-examination, he vowed to change. I had been working through mine for a few months, an intense exploration of how I got to be the way I am. We both ended up with an authentic desire to be the men God created us to be. Through the life of Jesús, I'd seen an image of myself. We each came to a moment of brokenness, and what we found there was God.

And He was enough.

We are all the same.

34. WHICH STORY?

Calls came in from major magazines—*Men's Journal, GQ,* the *New Yorker,* the *Sunday Times* of London. Each had assigned a reporter to write their own version of the story. During the interviews it was clear which writers had made up their minds about their angle— the spin they felt they needed to shape stories to appeal to their readers— long before they had met the fishermen or me. I understood that cannibalism and drug trafficking were sensational draws for readers, but I was dismayed that only one reporter attempted to learn about the fishermen themselves or discover the real truth of their ordeal. In fact, most of the interviews I did left me feeling as if I had been stabbed in the back.

Now I was taking it personally. I had spent enough time with the fishermen to have a sense of what their lives had been. No one from the press could ever really identify with that kind of life. All three of the fishermen had been born into extreme poverty. They had grown up without any guarantees of food, health care, or education. These were the *real* self-made men. A reporter would freak out just because the Wi-Fi at Starbucks wasn't working. Jesús,

Salvador, and Lucio dealt with real danger and real survival every day of their lives.

I set up a series of meetings with old friends from my TV days, hoping the smallness of Hollywood would allow me to step seamlessly into the movie neighborhood. (Oddly enough, this included the studio head of television whose job I had said I wanted all those years ago during my red-carpet days. He was now CEO at one of the smaller studios.)

After seeing the *Variety* article, he handed it to his staff. From that, one of his development people called me, asked how I had come to own the rights to the story, and wanted to know more about my ups and downs in getting it. I was already going to be in Los Angeles, so she invited me to meet and talk about a possible film project. I went to their offices in Santa Monica.

She asked again how I had come to own these story rights, and I told her a little bit of my personal story and how I'd gone to Mexico when the fishermen were returning home. Two other executives joined us. I told them the story of the fishermen, their survival, and their faith. When I was done, they all exchanged glances.

"Now tell them the other story," the woman said.

"What other story?" I didn't get it at first.

"The one about you."

I paused, felt awkward, but then stumbled into the "story of Joe." About two minutes in, they exchanged glances again in their all-powerful, all-knowing Hollywood way. I waited.

"That's act two," said one of them.

"What do you mean?" I asked him.

"It means this story of the fishermen needs a character like you," he said. "Three Mexican men on a boat speaking Spanish isn't a feature film; it's a documentary that nobody in the US will want to see. If we put a guy like you in the story, then guys like you will go see it."

"This is not about me," I said. "This is their story—their survival, their rescue, their faith. I can't be part of this."

"If you want anyone to see this movie," he said, "you'll have to get over that."

I left the meeting confused. The explanation for combining the two stories was only addressed in the context of profit. And while I understood the realities of commercial properties, in this case profit wasn't my primary driver—and still isn't.

At least I knew there was interest in the story. But now it bothered me that these guys thought three men surviving nine months at sea wasn't marketable, not unless my wacky life was tacked onto it.

A friend of mine called to give me the name of a reporter at the *Atlanta Journal-Constitution* who he thought should hear the story.

The reporter interviewed Carmen and me and sent a photographer, who took some shots of me wearing a warmup jacket and holding a Bible. My hair was a little long and mangy at the time, and I looked like an Old Testament track star. I didn't plan to represent Team Jesus this way; it's just what I happened to have on. The resulting pictures no doubt caused many a suburban wife to wonder how Carmen could have allowed me to appear before nearly one million readers without considering what kind of circus was happening on the top of my head.

The story was set to appear a week later, on January 21, 2007, on the front page of the Sunday edition. It must have been a slow news week.

The night before the story ran, I picked up my daughter and her friends from a swim meet and stopped at a convenience store to see if they had the early edition of the Sunday paper. There it was: a six-by-six-inch photo of me on the front page under the headline "A Test of Faith." All I can say is that it's bizarre to see yourself on the cover of anything. I picked up two more papers and resisted the urge to tell the cashier that you-know-who was on the cover.

Back in the car, I took a deep breath and handed a paper to my daughter and her friends.

"This is crazy, Dad," my twelve-year-old said. I took that to mean she was excited. But when she added, "It takes up the whole page," I realized she was really embarrassed.

To my daughters, this was unwanted notoriety. An image of their dad posing as an athletic, but slightly unkempt, religious zealot on the front page of the Sunday paper might cause some difficulties for them when they walked into school Monday morning.

Because of that article, I was invited to the Sundance Film Festival. I received an offer to do a film. For a short while, it was encouraging that there was such interest. But after closer examination, it seemed to me there were issues with each party who wanted to do the story as a movie. I didn't know much about the movie business, but I knew enough to understand when someone didn't "get" the spiritual journey that was core to the fishermen's experience.

I turned them down. The fishermen's story had to be told the way it deserved to be told.

35. His Stories

In each of the fishermen's villages, Masses were held to praise God for deliverance. Each liturgy was extraordinary in its own way, and the poignancy of these occasions was not lost on the celebrants who not long before had given the men up for dead.

Songwriters penned ballads about the fishermen, and amateur singers performed countless versions of the fishermen's story all over Mexico. They were becoming more than celebrities; they were also folk heroes whose ordeal of survival and faith was now canonized in songs.

It was odd for the fishermen. They went from the excruciatingly sluggish tick of the nearly twenty-five million endless seconds on the Pacific to the hypersonic pace of instant fame across several continents. It left little time to find a deeper meaning in all of it.

The manner in which the men spoke about themselves was subdued. As they talked, their words became simple declarative statements, which suggested they still couldn't quite believe it all had happened:

"We survived."

"We stayed alive."

"It was just day-to-day."

It was as if their past had its own life, separate and distant. It was over, far away, yet still a part of them:

"Not much we could do about the ending."

"We had faith."

It was simple. It was profound.

Generally the men wouldn't talk with strangers. When approached by someone they didn't know, the fishermen would become quiet. They were uncomfortable with all the compliments and well-wishing. They looked at their experience on the Pacific as what they had to do, and while faith was a part of that, so was drinking turtle blood and eating sharks. To them it wasn't a great accomplishment of faith, nor was it a great personal triumph of survival. It was what it was.

The songs and interviews and praise seemed odd to them.

Deep down inside the tough exteriors that are worn like armor, each man has a heart that is tender, that knows the truth.

For many, the fishermen's experience is beyond any realm of understanding, and because it doesn't fit into a compartment we can fathom, we question what is true. When you haven't experienced the miraculous, it's hard to get your arms around it. We are pretty wired to the ordinary. That's sad, because it leads us to dismiss the remarkable, the triumphant, the extraordinary, the supernatural. Those are compartments many of us don't have. As a result, we deprive ourselves of these dimensions to life.

So we look at the fishermen quizzically, probably similarly to the way people viewed a strange man who wandered down a mountain with his hair turned white and carrying stone tablets, and the crazy, hair-shirted, grasshopper-eating guy who dunked people in a river.

I believe Moses and John. And I believe the fishermen too.

36. "KEEP GOING!"

I spoke at the church of one of the men whom I had met on the Adventures of the Heart expedition. For me it was a kind of trial run, an early effort to tell the story to others effectively. My message was divided into two parts. I introduced myself and spoke briefly about my background and my own spiritual journey. Then I went into the real reason I was there, and I told the adventure story of the fishermen and their incredible survival. My personal story continued to be sort of an asterisk.

This was the first time I had told the story in public. I was given forty minutes. Sounds like plenty of time to pretty much tell anything. Well, it took me more than two hours. I didn't know it was going to take that long because I had never told the unabridged version before.

The reason I had only forty minutes was because this group met before the first church service. When my time was up, they were still sitting in their chairs. I wanted to be respectful of their time, so I stopped and said, "I know my time is up..."

"Keep going!" someone said.

I was surprised people were actually moved from hearing it. My story spilled into the church service time.

When the service ended, I still wasn't finished. Someone stopped me and said, "We don't want to leave, but some of us have to get our children from Sunday school." Kids were fetched, people returned, and the room filled with parents and children. We finally had to stop, but they invited me back.

After my return engagement, another two-hour session, a woman approached me. She said I was telling the story wrong. I thought this was a bit strange and more than a little bold, but I listened.

She said that this was one story, not two separate stories. She said my journey of faith was an essential part of the combined story. "The fishermen *looked* lost because they were in the middle of the Pacific Ocean with nothing but their faith," she said. "You, Joe, on the other hand, didn't *look* lost, because you had everything." Then she pointed out something I'd never thought of before: "But, Joe, in God's economy you *were* lost, whereas the fishermen were not lost at all. They had God."

I learned that she was a doctoral student whose concentration was in rhetoric and story. We met a few times a week over the next month or so, and she gave me advice about how to write all this. She was unrelenting in her belief that combining the two story lines—the fishermen's and mine—was the best approach.

I remained unconvinced. I didn't want my life story to intrude upon the more remarkable story of the fishermen. I wasn't even sure exactly what my story was, other than a man who went a little bit crazy, found God, and then spent a ton of money on a survival tale involving turtle blood on the Pacific. I couldn't imagine that my journey was of interest to anyone other than my therapist and me.

She kept pressing, and I kept dodging, and round and round we went each time we met. Even so, we made progress toward something I needed: getting the fishermen's story down on paper with a semblance of structure.

I expressed my reservations about the combined-story idea to a few of my close friends. They each started out agreeing with me, but as I shared the opinions of the studio and my PhD advisor-friend, they quickly shifted their opinion.

While their ideas echoed what I'd heard from the studio people earlier, they weren't focusing on the commercial value of anything, as the studios had been. They were saying there was something important and powerful in the two stories side by side, told in tandem, and woven together spiritually.

It slowly became clearer to me. I realized that although the process of trying to get a movie made had been chock-full of obstacles and rejection, God was somehow in it. I remembered how others had hinted at the second story, my story. It always seemed to come up.

And then my eyes were fully opened: God was present in all of it, speaking to me about what the story really was.

No, this isn't my story. But it isn't the fishermen's story either.

It is God's story, and *all* of what He has done needs to be told.

37. STANDING IN THE GAP

Carmen and I had a lot to work on—well, *I* had a lot to work on—and years of damage to understand and ask forgiveness for.

I had dropped everything and committed all that I had within me to telling this story. To be fair, Carmen had supported me beyond every reasonable expectation. She'd accepted that it was a spiritual quest I had to pursue. She'd held everything together while I was chasing the fishermen through the jungles of Mexico. But the story of the fishermen had taken all my time, consumed my energy, and was now starting to challenge us financially. Carmen felt that the project needed to be over, and she wanted our lives to get back to some shade of normal.

But my pursuit of the fishermen had finally landed the story, and I truly felt a responsibility to the three of them to see it to a fitting conclusion. Besides, *my* path to getting our finances whole again was to make a movie. I couldn't stop now, especially after I'd sunk so much money into it.

Our counselor, whom we had been seeing off and on for a while, had heard the two of us talk about this situation many times. I still wanted to go all out; Carmen was supportive but wary. At one point the counselor asked Carmen, "Can you be his cheerleader for one year?"

Carmen looked at me for a few moments before answering. "Yes, I suppose I can," she said.

Interesting how two people can interpret the same simple sentence so differently. I immediately felt a tremendous sense of relief. We were on the same team, and I was more confident than ever. What I heard was, "We're going all the way with this."

What Carmen heard, however, was, "If nothing concrete happens by December 31, 2007, at 11:59 p.m., then Joe agrees to drop the project so we can get on with our lives."

In fact, that was the agreement. I had a year to make something happen.

I spent most of that summer writing a screenplay and a rough draft of a book. Meanwhile, our savings shrank and the tension grew, although I was often oblivious to both. I really had no idea of the time needed to complete the project; also, I had no sense of how long it would take for money to come back in. My one year flew by. December 31 came and went. Nothing happened. Nothing moved forward. Yet I was still as confident as ever that what I was doing was God-ordained and that He would see it through.

Carmen felt betrayed. It didn't help that I told her I needed to go to the Sundance Film Festival *again*. She believed I was trying to do what I felt was God's will, but I know she sometimes wondered why God wasn't moving faster if this was what He really wanted. I'm sure Carmen sometimes prayed, "Lord, please make something happen or make it end."

I understood some of Carmen's concerns because I had my times of doubt too. Around that time a friend told me, "God can just as easily say yes to you or no to you now as He did when you were in Mexico."

Less than fifteen seconds later, I received this unsolicited e-mail from another friend:

Standing in the Gap

I looked for a man among them who would build up the wall
and stand before me in the gap on behalf of the land so I would
not have to destroy it, but I found none. —Ezekiel 22:30[5]

I had named my company Ezekiel 22 a year and a half before, because I had decided to stand in the gap.

My friend, who was sitting there with me, was as shocked as I was. I said simply, "I guess we'll keep going."

On many occasions it appeared that I was on the verge of making something happen with the movie. *This is it,* Carmen and I both thought each time. But many of these instances were mirages in the desert.

In fact, I did meet an up-and-coming director who loved the story of the fishermen and wanted to be part of it. And, of all the people I could have run across, he turned out to be an award-winning filmmaker from Greece who had recently become a Christian. But even though he was really interested, nothing happened. Still, I took this as another sign that I should stay the course.

Every time I came to the end of my rope—or I thought I had pushed Carmen to the end of hers—God would show me a sign of encouragement, though sometimes nothing more than the tiniest glimmer of hope. Still, I would eat it up, voraciously consuming even a little morsel. For Carmen, as accepting as she was, these tidbits were just teasers, accentuating the dire straits we were in.

We sold the lake house, which eased Carmen's mind a bit about our situation, even though she admitted she had loved our being there together as a family. To my way of thinking, selling the lake house bought me more time.

Over the next year I spent an inordinate amount of time with the Greek director, writing and rewriting the screenplay, leaving Carmen to take care of just about everything else in our lives. I knew she was angry during this period and thought I was being self-indulgent, but she somehow managed to affirm me in little ways.

Almost a full year after Carmen's "cheerleading" stint had expired, we had an exchange over transferring funds from one account to another so she could pay some bills. It was another unpleasant reminder that our finances were dwindling. As I worked on the draft of the screenplay, I composed this e-mail:

> Dear Carmen,
>
> Thank you, honey, for doing this. Pray for a miracle.
>
> Love,
> Your loser husband

She e-mailed me back:

> Joe,
>
> Praying is our best option. Let's hope that the cash truck turns down our street sooner rather than later. We have to tighten our belts.

By the way, you are not a loser. You have had a dream that you have followed for the last two years…that is not something a loser does. You have given it your all…that is not something a loser does. Keep the faith. Even if it does not come out in the end the way you planned it, haven't you enjoyed the journey?

You are smart, cute, and funny. 2009 will be full of new horizons. I just know it will be good!

Love you,
Carmen

Over the course of our marriage, Carmen had prayed that God would give her a godly man for a husband, and I think that was what sustained her during our toughest trials. She could see that I was genuinely seeking God with my whole heart, which is what Jesus said it would take to find Him.

Even so, I knew I had driven Carmen to the edge, and I continued to be fearful about the precariousness of our marriage.

I clung tightly to those e-mails like a frightened cat stranded on top of a telephone pole.

38. Wisdom and Folly

In the spring we had to sell Carmen's Lexus to cover some expenses, and I felt awful about it. Funny thing is, she had never wanted an expensive car. She would have been happy with a used Honda. I realized I had bought it for her to make *myself* feel better.

In mid-July our circumstances were starting to overwhelm us. We were broke. I had made a halfhearted effort to find a job. I wasn't resisting taking a job, but I believed if I turned my efforts away from what I felt God had led me to, I would be betraying Him. I was as discouraged as I had been since I discovered my faith in God.

Carmen had just about had it. We had garage sales and sold furniture, clothes, anything we didn't absolutely have to keep. I cashed in some of my life insurance policies. The IRS was contacting us about taxes and penalties due as a result of my draining the 401(k). The credit card companies started sending letters and calling, and the company that had financed one of our cars was threatening to repossess it—and eventually did, leaving us with just one car for the four drivers in our family.

While Carmen and I weathered these stresses together, they also created tensions between us.

I started praying more.

I added to my daily Bible readings a devotional, Oswald Chambers's *My Utmost for His Highest*. This classic work offered a short reading for each day. Short, but oh so profound. These daily nuggets would penetrate me to the core as if he were speaking directly to me.

The July 31 entry in that book haunted me:

> Not only must our relationship to God be right, but the external expression of that relationship must be right. Ultimately God will let nothing escape, every detail is under His scrutiny. In numberless ways God will bring us back to the same point over and over again. He never tires of bringing us to the one point until we learn the lesson, because He is producing the finished product.[6]

I went to a quiet place by the river near our house and mulled those words over and over. I prayed over them. I asked myself what my outward expression of my relationship with God was; turned out, it wasn't what I thought it should be.

And then it became crystal clear. What was the one point that God constantly brought me back to? *My marriage.*

My mind exploded with an extraordinary insight: *Is it possible that all along God was planning to use these circumstances to bless my marriage? Has He been laughing this whole time at my big plans for a movie and book?*

My increased time in prayer and Bible reading brought me to focus on the "wisdom books" of the Bible, two of which are Proverbs and Ecclesiastes. I had never focused on a set of books or themes from the Bible before, but I found myself especially drawn to Ecclesiastes and Proverbs as I tried to sort out why my life had become so chaotic. These books are all about wisdom and folly. I looked at it through the lens of Pass/Fail. I had a lot on the Fail list.

> Start with God—FAIL.
> Make insight your priority—FAIL.
> Don't assume you know it all—FAIL.
> Never take love for granted—FAIL.
> One who knows much says little—FAIL.

And only one on the Pass list:

> A wife of noble character—PASS.

That was the only one I got right.

How did I ever get so far away from being the man, husband, and father to her children that she deserved to have in her life?

What in the world was I thinking? That some sort of accomplishment, even in the name of God, could be a substitute for the nourishment, energy, and love my wife needed?

Did my performance-based upbringing have so much power in my life that I thought my accomplishments were the answer to her needs? How could I have been so misled? Deep inside me, and deep down inside most men, is a sensitive little boy hoping the exterior of a man will protect him. And the more we perform, the more we think we have built a wall of protection to keep that little boy from experiencing the pain we want to avoid at all costs.

I struggled putting these discoveries and feelings into words. So often my desires to serve God and to serve Carmen seem to compete with each other. "I can't do this without you," I told Carmen. "The torture is that I feel like I have to choose between the people I love and care about and what God has called me to, between the commitment I made to Him on that beach in Mexico and the vow I made to you on our wedding day. I just don't know what to do," I said in tears one day.

"You know I love you?" I asked.

"Yes," she said.

"You know that I have changed, right? My heart is different today." Carmen nodded. "You know that above all else I have to be obedient to Him, right?"

"Maybe you can do both," she said.

Do both? What a novel idea. *Why can't I do both? Why does everything have to be one or the other with me?* I wish I knew the answer to that. But just as important as the answer to that question is the fact that I recognize my tendency to be that way: all or nothing, black or white, fight or flight.

Soon after my report card of wisdom and folly, I confessed to Carmen how foolish I had been about so many things. She looked at me as if I were speaking Portuguese. But I could see the tenderness in her eyes as I talked about our marriage, our money, our health, and the folly of my life. I don't think she had seen this coming. I certainly didn't know I was going to say these things. Several seconds passed.

"Now I feel bad because you feel bad," she said finally.

"It's okay," I said. "It's a good kind of feeling bad." It allowed me to see her pain.

To my mind, Carmen and I had been in this together. But what I wasn't fully aware of before was that I had been the one out there flying fast and free: I was the kite, and she had been left holding the string.

The next Sunday, Carmen and I drove through rain to church, where we heard a sermon about taking responsibility for one's life.

Our pastor spoke of a phrase he used to hear his father say when he was a kid: "Later and greater." The message was simple: what we sow today, we reap later, and what we reap is always much greater than we expect it to be, which can be really good or really bad.

I thought about the seeds I'd sown. Some of the great ones are our two wonderful daughters. Carmen gets most of the credit for them.

Later in the car I said to Carmen, "I'm realizing that I've sown some lousy seeds in my life, especially in our marriage."

She sat looking straight out the windshield, holding in deep feelings.

"You've been reaping," I continued, "things you don't deserve."

The only sound was the rain pounding the roof of the car.

"I hope you can forgive me someday," I said. "I wouldn't blame you if you didn't."

I parked near the entrance of a grocery store, and I turned toward Carmen. "What I have tried to do," I said softly, "with this whole thing—with the fishermen—I've done with the purest intentions for them, and for us, and for our girls."

She didn't move.

"One of the reasons I am fighting so hard for this is so the kids will see their father as a man who is willing to take risks on things he says he believes in. I don't want to be a 'Don't do as I do; do as I say' father. I want to be a 'Do as I do' father."

Silence.

"I worry about the girls. What I've done. What I've not done. Those seeds I've sown. And now I'm praying this fishermen story and my connection to it might, one day, reap something better in them, greater than either of us could have imagined."

Carmen continued to stare straight ahead.

"I've started to think that maybe we had to go through all this to get to this point of healing in our marriage." I went on, "That we had to be stripped of everything so there was only us and God. No cushions. No insulation. No medicines. Not even the anesthetic of money to keep us from feeling the pain."

A tear ran down her cheek. Then another. Then a flood.

"I'm just tired," she said, sobbing. "I just want it to be over."

"I know."

"Why am I always the bad guy?" she asked, looking at me now.

I leaned over and put my hand on hers. "You're not," I said. "You're not to blame for any of this. You've been a rock, and you are the hero here."

Carmen nodded.

"Even if you decided you want out of this marriage, I wouldn't blame you," I said, squeezing her hand. "No matter what you do, I will always love you."

She wiped away tears from her cheeks. She looked out the window, her silence stark against the hum of the engine and the patter of the rain. I knew she was weighing everything.

After a moment she looked at me. A slight smile emerged. Carmen sighed and finally spoke. "Go get the groceries."

When she said that, it was music to my ears. I knew what it meant, because I knew Carmen. What a beautiful way to say "I will always love you too."

39. Seeds

Unexpectedly, our oldest daughter gave me the greatest gift a dad could receive, in the form of her essay for a scholarship:

To the Scholarship Committee:

The reason I am so dedicated to television production and communication studies is my dad. An executive in television for more than fifteen years, he facilitated the syndication of shows such as *Seinfeld, Mad About You,* and *Walker, Texas Ranger.* Ultimately, though, he left the corporate world behind to find something more—and what he found is the reason he is my hero.

For the past three years, he has been working to take a little-known story of hope and faith and tell it to as many people as possible. In 2006, three Mexican fishermen were rescued near the coast of Australia after being lost at sea in the

Pacific Ocean for more than nine months. When one of them was asked how they survived, he didn't respond with a tale of elaborate planning and fishing techniques—he simply pointed to his Bible.

My dad now has the rights to their story and has been working tirelessly to turn it into a book and a movie. His faith and dedication to this story inspires me every single day, but this work has taken a financial toll on our family. He has not had a salary in several years, yet he encouraged me to apply to this great university, knowing in his heart that it was the school of his daughter's dreams.

I would not be here today if it were not for him.

My daughter had written this from her heart. She had been watching. She had seen what I had hoped and prayed she would see. Three years earlier I didn't know how to make it available for her, but God did. He took the clay that had flown off the wheel and plopped it back down and started reshaping it.

She and her little sister are my legacy. Carmen's legacy. Our legacy. The seeds we had sown had become beautiful and vibrant in the form of our children.

They saw something I lose track of sometimes. They saw my faith. They saw their mom's faith. They saw the faith of the fishermen. They saw the faithfulness of God.

And they saw healing and restoration. It is being lived out in front of them. It is something greater than I could have ever imagined.

40. BUOYANT

Carmen and I awoke one morning, sensing something new in the air.

She gave me her to-do list for the day, and we ran errands. We spent the afternoon together in the one car we had left. She laughed. I laughed.

"I like this," I said after about an hour of driving her around.

"Maybe you should get a job as a chauffeur," she said.

"No. I mean I like hanging out with you, doing nothing, together. I could see us doing this on a regular basis."

She looked over at me. "Me too," she said.

That evening we had another session with our counselor.

"So, how are you two doing?" he asked.

There was the usual awkward silent moment where we look at each other, knowing that whoever speaks first is the one in the cross hairs. "Great!" I finally said. Carmen agreed.

"Tell me what that means," he said. I told him about the weekend and the conversation that had started in the church parking lot and ended at the grocery store, how I admitted I had been foolish and how Carmen had cried, about the freshness of the day and the sense of renewal, about the feeling of joy and connectedness I had while I was playing chauffeur. Carmen agreed.

"Congratulations!" he said. "Sixteen sessions and you've finally de-escalated the negative dynamic of the dance of your power struggle."

Carmen and I looked at each other and smiled. We just thought we were having a good day.

The counselor went on to explain how difficult it is to break this cycle. He explained that restoration was on its way.

I felt a nudge and again apologized to Carmen for all the times I was insensitive and self-absorbed. As I did this, I thought, *I don't ever want to get so far away from being the man, husband, and father to her children that she deserves to have in her life.* I think she could feel the authenticity of my sorrow for having caused her so much heartache.

Carmen looked deep into my eyes, tears welling. "It is so nice to finally hear you acknowledge how painful this has been for me," she said. "It makes me want to for—"

She stopped, collected herself, and started again.

"It *allows* me to forgive you."

Epilogue

The fishermen were rescued in 2006. They have yet to see the movie of their epic ordeal. We will never give up on this.

The events of their survival and return have changed them. And yet in other ways, much has remained the same. They have settled back into their lives as fishermen, much as before, except now each has a boat of his own.

When the fishermen floated across the Pacific Ocean, wondering if survival was in the cards, time moved slowly. When they got back to land, time seemed to speed up. The realization that there was a finite amount of time left for them set in. That happens when death stares at you every day. Making every moment count becomes a lifestyle.

Once they were back in Mexico, they went about routines that looked similar to the things they did before, but there was more urgency in their lives. Spending time with friends and family became more important, more precious. Helping others is now a common activity in their lives.

These became new priorities for the men whose names literally translate to "Jesus," "Savior," and "Light."

JESÚS

Today, Jesús has become a generous man. He bought uniforms for a local soccer team. He purchased a pacemaker for a boy in his village. It is a different life for him now.

Local leaders wanted him to be mayor. They didn't ask him to run for mayor. They just said, "You are going to be mayor." He respectfully declined. At the core Jesús is a servant, as evidenced by his loyal position as number two for nine months on the ocean.

Jesús has also become an example of personal change. He is becoming the husband and father he was created to be. It is, in another way, heroic.

I have learned from his example.

SALVADOR

Today, Salvador remains an emblem of strength and determination in the face of uncertain times.

He was built and prepared by God to be the strength of the three fishermen. On the ocean, as soon as he assessed how impossible the situation was, he turned to God. Armed with the two most important survival tools in the world—his faith and his Bible—he was prepared to give a heroic daily fight that would have continued to the death if necessary.

Like Daniel in the Bible, he was inextricably connected to God's power during the ordeal. He surrendered the outcome of their situation to the hands of God and got to work with the business at hand, believing that even if they died, it didn't change who God was.

Today, Salvador continues to have an uncomplicated and unwavering faith.

He has no idea how much his character has influenced me. I constantly consult his example of faith in my own circumstances.

LUCIO

Lucio is a miracle to his family. He is called "born again" by those who had buried him.

Today he has finally accepted that "city people" can never understand his survival at sea. His life is very much the same as before, and even though he was given a boat to start his own fishing enterprise, he says that he has no business running a business. He is not interested in traveling or having a home of his own. He prefers the simplicity of living with his Panchita in San Blas and being thankful God has given him life.

Lucio has had many blessings, including his discovery that it is possible to reconnect with family members and heal the hurts.

In this, I find my own connection with him.

Lucio also has something going for him that we all wish we could have. He has the power of a praying grandmother, and her dreams of him living as an example to his family have come true.

PANCHITA

Panchita, the matriarch of a family filled with fishermen, today maintains the humble and unswerving faith she's had for many years. She did not succumb to the worst but held on to the best. Her refusal to give up hope for Lucio didn't look rational to the rest of the family. Setting a place for him at the table for dinner every night looked very much like a form of denial.

But her faith not only sustained her; it may have been responsible for Lucio's survival and rescue. With her daily prayers for his safety, she did what many grandmothers do for their children and grandchildren—she got her family through the most difficult times of their lives by praying for them "without ceasing."[7]

CARMEN AND JOE

Today, I'm happy to say we are more alive than ever. Our lives are certainly not perfect, but Carmen and I are in the best place we have been in years. We are blessed with a faith that has been a sustaining force in all we do and all we face. We have a roof over our heads, our girls are healthy, and the trajectory of their lives has changed in tremendously important ways. We thank God for all of it.

Carmen continues to be a rock, and she still looks like a rock star. When I asked her to marry me and she said yes, it took 1.4 seconds. But her vow of "I do" was forever. "Till death do us part," she said. And she meant it. She stayed with me. She is my hero.

The two of us watched the Oscars this year. Seeing the ceremony brought back memories of when I once stood on a red carpet in Hollywood. I recalled the memory as if it were yesterday: the celebrities, the early evening sun illuminating the glitz and glamour. But watching it again was also a shock to me as I was confronted with how much has happened since that night in 1997. I thought I had so much back then—wealth and success—yet how impoverished I was.

Today, on the outside I might still look like the guy who "arrived" that evening on the red carpet, but not on the inside. I have been showered with grace. That grace has restored me—not to my former life, but to the fullness I chased after and never found, a rich life that now includes Carmen's love, the esteem of my two precious girls, and the awesome pleasure of God.

When a man is restored in this way, he wants to share it with others; he *needs* to share it with others. And now, as I share my story, I feel deep connections to those around me. I see pain in the eyes of other men. I want them to know there is healing, no matter how deep their hurt is or how distant re-demption may seem. I see desperate hope in the eyes of women who have remained strong for so long that they have forgotten what it's like to breathe a sigh of relief from it all. I want them to know that God rescues men and brings them back.

We're all on journeys like the three fishermen. I could say we are all struggling and surviving much as they did. But in the end I can only speak for myself, how I came to faith in God and how He rescued me. I can say I have looked into the eyes of Jesús and Salvador and Lucio, and I've seen my-self. If in my whole life, my whole journey, I've learned anything, it is this:

I am the fourth fisherman.

ACKNOWLEDGMENTS

There are so many to thank. First, to my wife, Carmen, and my daughters, who love me in spite of myself, thank you, thank you, thank you. To my incredible agent, Bonnie Solow, who found me and believed the story was something special. My editor, Ken Petersen, who drew out of me what I didn't know existed. Lee Strobel for his kind words. Everyone at Random House, Crown Books, and WaterBrook Multnomah, who are amazingly skilled at what they do. Joshua, whose prayers started me on this journey with the Creator, and Allison, his wife, who is my friend, my writer's helper, and the funniest person I know. My first editor, Al, who helped keep an economy of words. Ralf, who provided helpful notes and research. Howard, who has been there through thick and thin. My friend Victoria, who introduced me to the story of the fishermen and prayed for my safety, knowing that it was probably more dangerous than I ever realized. Her nephew Eli, who helped me not only with translation but also with prayer. All those who helped me in Mexico: Armando, Josefina, Silverio, Eduardo, David, and the staff at Casa Mañana. All those who have shared their treasure to help advance this story: Rocky, David, Bert, Fran, Chris, John, Charlie, Van, Keith, and Todd. Reed, who is responsible for getting this book finished by kicking me in the behind. Marty, Julie, and Tyler for their artistic touch. Andrew, the best guy I ever hired. Bill, for his keen eye. Don, Spiros, and Rodrigo, who all have worked to get a movie of this story made. Everyone in my small groups: Keith, Todd, Charlie, and John. Their wives: Leigh, Celia, Kay, and Susan. Mark and Alice, Van and Susan, Reid and Hope, and Frank and Susie. The group of guys I met through Adventures of the Heart. Our pastor, Andy, and his father, Charles, and everyone at North Point and In Touch Ministries, who are so gifted at being messengers of the Word. Jeff and Billy and the staff at Buckhead Church for doing all you do to lead people into the most important relationship they will ever have. Paige, Betsy, Beth, Tammy, and Hannah, for watching over my babies as friends and mentors. Gabe and his crew, who are amazing with their connector skills. Paul, for showing me that there really is no business model for this kind of thing. *God is the model.* For all those who let us use their homes to think and write: Keith, Lever, Mark, Ron, and Deborah. Cec, Fox, Bart, Shaunti, and Jeff, for the contribution of their words. My friends and colleagues who are part of old Joe—what I like to call BC—Terry, Barry, Ed, Susan, Steve, John, and Greg. My mom and dad. You did the best you could. It was hard, I know, and I am thankful that you stayed together for my sake for all those years. My sister, Jan, and my brother Jay. My brother Jeff, who left us too soon. My in-laws, Don and Millie. My brother-in-law, Jeff, who helped me get started. The tens of thousands of people who prayed for us, loved us, introduced us to someone we needed to meet, supported our efforts in all this, and chose to be our friends.

Finally, and above all else, Father, Son, and Holy Spirit, who love me, guide me, and dwell in me. They gave me a second life, which I certainly didn't deserve.

NOTES

1. Scott P. Richert, "Tuesday Prayer for the Faithful Departed," Weekly Prayers for the Souls in Purgatory, Catholicism, About.com, http://catholicism.about.com/od/prayers/qt/Prayer_Dead_Tue.htm.

2. "Fishermen: We Never Gave Up Hope to Be Saved, MSNBC.com, August 18, 2006, www.msnbc.msn.com/id/14410580/ns/world_news-americas/t/fishermen-we-never-gave-hope-be-saved.

3. Maria Mackay, "Lost Fishermen Survived Thanks to Fish and Faith," *Christianity Today,* August 23, 2006, www.christiantoday.com/article/lost.fishermen.survived.thanks.to.fish.and.faith/7340.htm.

4. verses 6, 9, MSG

5. NIV

6. Oswald Chambers, *My Utmost for His Highest* (Uhrichsville, OH: Barbour, 1935), July 31.

7. 1 Thessalonians 5:17, KJV

SPREADING HOPE

THE FOURTH FISHERMAN

Blog • Video • Events • Resources

Email
joe@ezekiel22.com

Facebook
Facebook.com/joekissack

Twitter
Twitter.com/joekissack

More information at TheFourthFisherman.com